isbn #: 1-57440-008-8   Copyright 1997   Primary Research Group, Inc.

TABLE OF CONTENTS

Primary Research Group, Inc.   P.O. Box 20853, New York, NY 10023   212/397-5055

LIST OF TABLES

Primary Research Group, Inc.   P.O. Box 20853, New York, NY 10023   212/397-5055

4

Primary Research Group, Inc.   P.O. Box 20853, New York, NY 10023   212/397-5055

Primary Research Group, Inc.   P.O. Box 20853, New York, NY 10023   212/397-5055

Primary Research Group, Inc.   P.O. Box 20853, New York, NY 10023   212/397-5055

Primary Research Group, Inc.   P.O. Box 20853, New York, NY 10023   212/397-5055

Primary Research Group, Inc.   P.O. Box 20853, New York, NY 10023   212/397-5055

Primary Research Group, Inc.   P.O. Box 20853, New York, NY 10023   212/397-5055

11

Primary Research Group, Inc.   P.O. Box 20853, New York, NY 10023   212/397-5055

CHAPTER ONE: INTRODUCTORY MATERIALS

INTRODUCTION

This report is based on a survey of 44 college distance education programs chosen from a list of such programs compiled from an amalgamation of sources. Respondents were asked to provide quantitative and qualitative answers to questions regarding a broad range of issues about their programs. The full questionnaire is reproduced Appendix I. Generally, these questions concern budgeting, marketing, course development, instructor training and compensation, program range, technologies used, market demographics and other issues of interest to college administrators and program suppliers.

WHY IS DISTANCE LEARNING SPREADING?

In the recent past, and still to some extent today, correspondence education enjoyed a reputation in the academic pecking order somewhat above mud wrestling and roller derby and somewhat below traditional academic education. Slowly, however, new technologies, and new concerns in academia for efficiency in the educational process, have combined to open the door for distance learning to become a major force in higher education in America. Other factors have also played a role in the gradual opening of the academic door to distance learning. Governors of key states have pushed distance learning as a way to control escalating higher education costs. Experiments in distance learning conducted by major corporations and government agencies have shown that distance learning is -- for many applications -- a less expensive but just as effective way to teach certain kinds of material as traditional classroom education.

The astounding growth of the internet, and the gradual though steady increase in the personal computer usage in the general population has also been a catalyst. The deregulation of telecommunications markets, and the surge of new telecom technologies, has also helped shake the mud off of distance education and enshrine it as a technologically advanced, cool and academically sexy thing to be involved with. Successful use of distance education in Canada, Australia and the UK has also led many American colleges (that already compete in world education markets with these countries for foreign students) to take another look at distance education.

The World Bank and the United Nations have taken up the banner of distance education. The US Department of Energy and the Pentagon have touted its effectiveness. IBM trains some of its employees at a distance. The academic world has listened to the chorus and is developing its own approach.

The impetus for increased use of distance learning in higher education as a way to control costs is being pioneered more by public colleges than private ones, and particularly by public colleges in the West, especially the West Coast and Rocky Mountain states. The largest increase in enrollment over the next fifteen years will occur in these public colleges, and they are anxious to reduce per student education costs and have become, to some extent, a workshop for new education technologies. A higher percentage of the total population seeks college education in the West, and a higher percentage of students are educated at public colleges than in the South, East or Midwest. Moreover, the western states are growing rapidly, and demographic and economic growth are generally, with some exceptions, faster than elsewhere in North America. Consequently, as the mini-baby boom demographic bulge starts entering colleges in the West of the United States, these states will feel more pressure than others to make their state universities as efficient as possible.

Over the past four years, there has been a rush in the West to create "virtual" educational institutions; organizations which bring together a wide swath of educational programs and courses and electronically deliver them to students. California is actively involved in planning a California Virtual University. Established and supported by Governor Pete Wilson, this new organization will include 106 community colleges, the 23-campus California State University system, the nine campuses of the University of California, Stanford, the University of Southern California, and Cal Tech. Parallel to that effort, the Cal State System is also planning a virtual university, designed to electronically provide CSU courseware from the system's 23 campuses.

Eleven institutions of the CSU are offering degree or certificate programs over the internet. The summary notes that "Most campuses are using their offices of Continuing/Extended Education (CE/EE) to lead the development of internet programs. On many of these campuses, the efforts of the CE/EE are assisted by other campus units assigned to assist with instructional development using television and other technology-supported media. On a few campuses, the primary responsibility rests with campus units outside the CE/EE.

Governors of 10 western states have formed Western Governor's University, a virtual university that will be a degree-granting, accredited institution.

The governors' plan to move the virtual university through several steps, starting with the offering of courses in a restricted number of disciplines at the college level, and culminating with a full scale university.

In the East, the University of Maryland has been particularly active, leading a consortium of more than 50 colleges and universities that are developing distance education courses. Several states have entered into arrangements with telecommunications providers to provide distance learning networks through wire and satellite links. In addition, many other state university systems have formed units specializing in distance learning, and are beginning to use distance learning beyond its traditional employment. The traditional uses of distance learning have been to allow students that face some kind of geographic, physical or time-related barrier to traditional college education. Major end users of distance education from colleges have been: 1) the chronically sick or disabled, or those entrusted with the day to day care of disabled or chronically-ill individuals, 2) people in remote geographic regions such as certain part of Alaska, Pacific Islands, or the Dakotas in the USA, who might be more than a hundred miles or more from the nearest facility of higher education suitable to their needs, 3) incarcerated individuals, 4) individuals with dramatic time constraints, such as a single mother raising three small children. Increasingly, however, state universities are developing distance learning alternatives for populations that find distance learning merely convenient rather than absolutely essential, or that find distance learning formats superior to traditional education formats, since distance learning can actually allow for more interaction with instructors via e-mail.

Community colleges are also being particularly aggressive in their pursuit of distance education alternatives. World Community College, a virtual community college, is already up and running. WCC is a consortium of colleges that offer courses on-line. The WCC offers all of the traditional accoutrements of a "physical" 2-year college including financial aid and libraries. The WCC was formed through an alliance between Community Colleges for International Development (CCID) and Electronic University Network (EUI), a private concern, located in San Francisco. Many community colleges are setting up distance training programs for particular companies, particularly medium-sized companies 100 to 1000 employees, that do not have extensive training or education departments, but have outgrown the casual, in-house training common in smaller concerns. Community colleges in the Pacific Northwest appear particularly active.

CHARACTERISTICS OF THE SURVEY RESPONDENTS

Of the colleges surveyed, more than half, 51.4%, had fewer than 250 students enrolled in their distance education programs. Fewer, 37.8%, had between 250 and 1,000 students enrolled in DE courses, while only 10.8% had more than 1,000 students.

Table #1: Number of Students Enrolled in The Distance Education Programs of the Surveyed Colleges.

Fewer Than 250	Between 250 and 1,000	More Than 1,000
51.4%	37.8%	10.8%

Of the colleges surveyed, 21% were located in the West; 34.8% in the South; 14% in the Northeast; and 30.2% in the Midwest.

Table #2: Percentage of Colleges Surveyed in Different Regions of The United States.

West	South	Northeast	Midwest
21%	34.8%	14%	30.2%

Primary Research Group, Inc.   P.O. Box 20853, New York, NY 10023   212/397-5055

The colleges surveyed were divided almost evenly into junior and senior colleges, with only 11.6% fewer junior colleges.

Table #3: Percentage of the Number of Colleges Surveyed
That Were Junior Colleges or Senior Colleges.

Junior Colleges	Senior Colleges
44.2%	55.8%

The mean number of total students (full and part-time) attending the colleges in the sample was 7,950; the median number, 5,300.

The mean number of part time students attending the colleges in the sample was 3,065; the median number, 1,700.

The mean number of full time students attending the colleges in the sample was 4,565; the median number, 3,300.

One of the colleges in the sample was a graduate school only, while another one was a seminary.

Seven percent of the colleges in the total sample were technical colleges.

SUMMARY OF SOME MAJOR FINDINGS

95.3% of the colleges with an established distance education program plan to expand the program.

44.2% of colleges with an established distance education program offer a full degree program through distance education.

75% of colleges with more than 1,000 students enrolled in an established distance education program offer a full degree program through distance education.

36.8% of colleges with less than 250 students enrolled in a distance education program offer a full degree program through distance education.

23.3% of colleges with established distance education programs attempt to sell or license distance learning services to other organizations.

4.7% of colleges with established distance education programs have sold a DE course to an organization in a developing country.

51.2% of colleges with established distance education programs have made an effort to assess the market demand for DE courses.

40% of college distance education programs operate at a loss. 25% of such programs operate with a profit margin of less than 10% above costs while another 25% operate with a profit margin between 11% and 30% above costs. 10% of distance education programs earn between 31% and 50% above costs.

42.5% of colleges with established distance education programs compensate instructors for course development on a regular basis; 47.5% do not. 10% of colleges with established distance education programs sometimes compensate DE instructors for course development.

In 65.8% of colleges with an established distance education program, the teaching load of a DE instructor is the same as that of a traditional classroom instructor. It is higher than that of a traditional classroom instructor in 23.7% of colleges and lower in only 10.5% of colleges.

Formal training is required of DE instructors in 52.6% of junior colleges with established distance education programs and in 56.5% of senior colleges with established distance education programs.

Students enrolled in distance learning courses received training in 26.3% of junior colleges with a distance education program in place and in 60.9% of colleges otherwise with a distance education program in place.

The mean percentage of distance education instructors that are adjunct faculty was 27.34%; the median 15%.

The mean fee for developing a distance learning course was $826.00. The base for calculating this average includes those colleges that do not pay instructors for developing distance learning courses.

The mean number of distance education courses offered by the schools surveyed was 35.07; the median number, 22. The minimum number of courses offered was 2; the maximum 200.

Many distance learning programs are slowly "feeling their way", experimenting with ways to reach organize programs and reach students. Survey participants interviewed for this report often stressed that distance learning is an open book, it is what you make it, and it definitely requires gradually traveling down the learning curve. The educational efficiency of distance learning programs improves with practice and perhaps the first rule is not to be afraid to try new approaches, but to quickly eliminate what does not work and retain (and spread knowledge of) what does work.

At its best, distance learning compels instructors to anticipate what their students will not understand, the extent to which they don't understand it, and what can be done to quickly help them overcome their confusion. Distance learning compels instructors to anticipate failure so that they can develop approaches through tape, interactive voice response, internet or other means that effectively leads to better educational results with less teacher manpower.

Most programs are relatively small, appeal to older, married, handicapped or other students with a time/space constraint, focus on relatively technical subjects with quick economic pay offs. Colleges and universities are beginning to put together programs (formal and informal) to train instructors, but most initiatives consist of short four to six hour instructor orientation sessions, along with manuals, booklets and web pages devoted to DE instruction training.

Course development appears to be relatively ad hoc although many colleges give instructors grants to develop DE courses, and assistance from other departments of the college (such as computer programming) that can be of assistance. A market has developed for DE courses, and the purchase (and sale) of DE courses has become more common, though most colleges seem to be developing their own courses at this point. Although Primary Research Group does not suspect that in the short term the sale of DE courses to the higher education market will be a very lucrative venture for colleges that develop effective DE courses, it is probably worthwhile at this point for some of the more active an innovative programs to explore marketing opportunities, either alone, in conjunction with other colleges, or in association with private sector education content publishers and telecommunications suppliers, many of whom have taken an interest in this market. Information on some of these publishers can be found in "The Adult and Continuing Education Business Report," also published by Primary Research Group.

The ratio of salaried instructors to adjuncts (defined as teachers that are not salaried instructional employees of the college and receive compensation on a per course of per student enrolled basis) is higher in distance learning than in traditional college classes. Although many adjuncts teach distance learning classes, salaried employees predominate, and we suspect that many DE programs get their start with moonlighting salaried teachers accepting an extra class in a distance learning program. In time, we suspect that adjuncts will be used more extensively, once a pool of acceptable candidates develops. At this point, however, it seems that a student is more likely to get a salaried instructor in a distance learning setting than in a traditional class.

We expect a second wave of distance learning interest to stem from college departments. Currently, most initiatives seem to be promoted by the college administration. However, since distance learning is viewed primarily as a way to serve new markets, and not really as a way to serve the traditional 18-24 year old predominantly non-married college youth population (although this may change), traditional departmental administration will come to view it, not as a threat, but as an opportunity to expand their programs. This is particularly true of faculties in business, engineering, computer science, nursing and other career-oriented disciplines.

This report was not intended as a market research report. The sample was drawn from existing programs, not from the overall universe of American colleges and universities. Primary Research Group suspects that a survey drawn from this universe would show that many colleges are now in the planning stages of developing distance learning programs. In addition, 95% of the 44 programs in the sample plan on program expansion, suggesting very rapid market growth for suppliers of equipment and programming.

In a rough way, the equipment market might be divided into four segments; broadcast approaches, videoconferencing approaches, internet-based approaches, and traditional correspondence, often supplemented by voice or other telecommunications technologies. Videoconferencing and the internet hold the most immediate promise; the former for educational efficacy, the latter, for convenience and low cost. However, the data clearly shows that no single technology predominates. The playing field is still relatively open -- any one technology could still make dramatic gains. Most potential equipment purchasers are experimenting; brand loyalties, and loyalties to particularly technologies are relatively weak, but not non-existent.

CHAPTER TWO: THE ADMINISTRATIVE STRUCTURE OF DISTANCE EDUCATION PROGRAMS

The encouragement and stewardship of distance education programs in higher education in the United States comes predominantly from the executive administration of the college. Although many distance education administrators work within specific academic departments, a slight majority identify their positions as within the executive administration of the college. Of the institutions surveyed, 51.2% of distance education administrators see themselves primarily as part of the executive administration; 46.5% as part of a traditional departmental administration; 23.3% as part of the faculty; and 11.6% as part of another, unnamed, corner of the institution.

The categories below are not completely mutually exclusive.

Table # 4: The Position of Distance Education Administrators
In the Hierarchy of the Institution.

	Executive Administration	Traditional Departmental Administration	Faculty	Other
Percentage	51.2%	46.5%	23.3%	11.6%

The overwhelming majority of distance education administrators report directly to the university administration, as table #5 below shows. Distance education is still a highly centralized, administration-inspired phenomena. The data suggests (and suggest is the correct word, not prove or even imply) that distance education has not been fully embraced by the faculty at large. Distance education seems to be a "top-down" revolution, perhaps promoted more by the administration than the professorial rank and file.

Table #5: Person or Department to whom Distance Education
Administrators Report.

	Academic Department Chairmen	University Administration	Special Distance Learning Department	Other
Percentage	9.3%	86%	4.7%	0%

Primary Research Group, Inc.   P.O. Box 20853, New York, NY 10023   212/397-5055

Distance Education programs are viewed primarily as a way to serve special populations, though almost half of the colleges surveyed indicated that they are also considered to be an integral part of traditional degree programs.

The following categories are not mutually exclusive.

Table #6: How Distance Education Programs are viewed from Within the Institution.

View	A Profit-Making Function	An Integral Part of Traditional Degree Programs	A Way to Serve Special Populations	Other
Percentage	11.6%	46.5%	79.1%	4.7%

Interestingly, only a relatively small percentage of distance learning programs serve a "national" market; indeed, nearly as many serve the international market. Most are regional or local in nature, as table #7 relates.

Table #7: Markets Served by Distance Education Programs.

	Local Market	Statewide Market	National Market	International Market	Regional Market
Percentage of programs serving various markets	69.8%	53.5%	30.2%	25.6%	46.5%

As shown in table #8 on the following page, the university administration directly receives revenues from a little less than half of all programs; approximately another half send revenues to some other administrative unit, such as an academic department or special distance education unit.

Table #8: Recipients of Revenue From Distance Education Courses.

	Traditional Academic Department*	Adult or Continuing Education Program	Separate Unit Devoted to Distance Learning	The University Administration	Other
Percentage	23.3%	11.6%	18.6%	46.5%	23.3%

*This may include adult or continuing education

We asked survey participants to comment on the destination of revenues from the DE program, and these responses are cataloged below:

*The DE effort is not independent of the rest of the college academic degree program. It is currently bringing in more money than budgeted.

*The revenue from DE courses goes to a separate unit devoted to distance learning, the university administration, and department support offices (library, computer center, student services)
    -- University with more than 15,000 students

*The revenue from DE courses goes to the college operating budget.
    -- Senior college with fewer than 5,000 students

*Revenue from DE courses is put into the general fund of the budget, like any other tuition or fees.
    -- Junior college with between 5,000 and 15,000 students

*Revenue from DE courses goes to the general revenue fund distributed by the administration.
    -- University with between 5,000 and 15,000 students

*Revenue from DE courses goes to Graduate Studies.
    -- Senior college with between 5,000 and 10,000 students

* Revenue from DE courses goes to the general fund.
    -- Senior college with more than 15,000 students

* Revenue from the DE courses is not treated differently from other funds; it goes into the general revenue fund of the college.

The majority of distance education programs use instructors that are paid as part of their regular load, though more than half use instructors that are paid as an overload or as an adjunct. Only one in five use instructors that are paid on a per student basis.

Table #9: The Administrative Organizarion of Payment.

Method of Payment	Part of Load	Overload	Per Student	As Adjunct*
Percentage of Colleges That Pay any DE Instructors	74.4%	53.5%	20.9%	51.2%

*This includes tenured or other regularly employed faculty that may be paid as adjuncts to teach an additional course, as well as regular adjuncts. Some colleges, indeed most in the sample, use adjuncts as well as salaried instructors in their DE programs.

Course design is still relatively ad hoc in most programs, and table ten shows no truly dominant course design mechanism or procedure.

Table #10: How Courses Are Designed.

	Some Kind Of Centralized DE Faculty or facility	Through Grants to Regular Faculty	Purchased From Outside Source	Other
Percentage	16.3%	23.3%	14%	53.5%

Primary Research Group, Inc.   P.O. Box 20853, New York, NY 10023   212/397-5055

We asked survey participants to comment on the support that they receive in course design from other departments of the college. Their responses are listed below:

*Instructional design, graphics, and other media production instructional technologist (M.S.) are on staff as support services offered for faculty designing courses for distance ed.
    -- Junior College

* Support services offered to faculty designing courses include, instructional designers, graphic artists, html programmers, professional teaching skills and use of technology.
    -- University with more than 15,000 students

* Support services offered to faculty designing courses for distance ed. include instructional designers and html programmers.
    -- Senior College

* Support services offered for faculty designing courses are a template and the service of a webmaster.
    -- Graduate School

* Support service offered to faculty designing courses consists of a graphic artist.
    -- Junior College with fewer than 5,000 students

* Support services offered: Html programmers.
    -- Junior College with fewer than 5,000 students

* Support services offered to faculty designing courses for distance ed. consist of workshops.
    -- Senior College with fewer than 5,000 students

* Students help in the area of support services as instructional designers, graphic artists, html programmers, etc.
    -- University with between 5,000 and 15,000 students

* Support services offered to faculty designing courses for distance ed. consists of laptop computers, list-serve assistance, powerpoint instruction and help through the instructional technology center on campus.
    -- University with more than 15,000 students

* Support services offered to faculty designing courses for distance ed. consist of graphic artists.
    -- Senior College with between 5,000 and 15,000 students

* An AV production specialist is offered as a support service to faculty designing courses for distance ed.
    -- Junior College with fewer than 5,000 students

* Instructional designers, graphic artists, and html programmers are all offered to faculty as support services in designing courses.
    -- Junior College with fewer than 5,000 students

* No support services are offered to faculty designing courses.

* Graphic artists are offered as support service to faculty designing DE courses.
    -- Junior College with between 5,000 and 15,000 students

* Instructional designers, graphic artists, and html programmers can be available to faculty designing courses, if needed.
    -- University with between 5,000 and 15,000 students

* No support services are offered to distance education instructors designing distance education courses.
    -- University with more than 15,000 students

* Assistance to distance education instructors designing distance education courses is provided through the other areas of the college.
    -- Junior College with between 5,000 and 15,000 students

* Support services offered to distance education instructors include faculty discussion of instructional issues, and an on-line teaching guide.

* One on one from support staff as required and requested is offered to faculty designing courses for distance education.
    -- Junior College with between 5,000 and 15,000 students

* Instructional designers, graphic artists, and html programmers are offered to faculty designing courses as support services.

* Support services offered to faculty include technicians on-site during all sessions, and instructional designers.
    -- Senior College with fewer than 5,000 students

* Support services for faculty designing distance education programs includes the computer department staff and the media production coordinator
    -- Seminary

* Support services offered to faculty designing courses for distance education include the Coordinator of Distance Education, Instructional Support personnel, and computer programmers.
    -- Senior College with fewer than 5,000 students

* We help them learn these skills [instructional designers, graphic artists, html programmers] for them to do it.]
    -- Senior College with between 5,000 and 15,000 students

* Support services offered to faculty designing courses for distance education include Learning Technologies Consultant staff from Computing Services.

* No support services are offered for faculty designing distance education courses.
    -- Senior College with more than 15,000 students

* Support services for distance education instructors designing courses for distance ed. include graphic designers and a curriculum specialist. We are at this time looking for funding to employ instructional designers and html programmers.

* Support services offered to faculty designing courses consist of the faculty collaborating with a curriculum development professional at Canter Educational Productions.

* Instructional designers are offered as a support service for distance educators designing distance education classes.
    -- Junior College

* For support services, aiding distance educators in designing distance education classes, the university has limited access to instructional design/graphics that the entire university uses. Departments must pay for programming assistance.
    -- University with more than 15,000 students

* Instructional designers, graphic artists, and html programmers are offered to faculty designing courses as support services.

* Services offered to distance education instructors designing distance education courses include a course editor, and a webmaster.

We also asked survey participants to comment on which department or division of the college actually designs the DE courses. Some additional comments on this issue appear below.

* Courses are designed by a college curriculum committee.
    -- Junior College

* Courses are designed in a centralized faculty.
    -- University with more than 15,000 students

* Courses are designed by tech support people.
    -- Senior College

* All courses created adhere to a standardized template.
    -- Graduate School

* Courses are designed on faculty's own time or through curriculum development funds.
    -- Senior College with between 5,000 and 15,000 students

* Courses are designed at school and at home.
    -- University with between 5,000 and 15,000 students

* Faculty design their own courses.
    -- Senior College with fewer than 5,000 students

* Courses are developed from faculty recommendations by a faculty/administrative team.
    -- Junior College with more than 15,000 students

* Courses are designed based on courses already given on campus.
    -- University

* Courses are designed by individuals receiving course releases to do so.
    -- Senior College with fewer than 5,000 students

* The courses are equivalent to the on-campus offerings with slight modifications to deliver them at a distance.
    -- Senior College with fewer than 5,000 students

* Courses, except for telecourses, which are purchased from outside sources, are designed through grants to the faculty

* Courses are jointly designed by faculty and Canter Educational Productions and then produced by Canter, for us.

* Courses are designed by individual faculty.
    -- University with more than 15,000 students

* Distance education courses are designed by faculty.
  -- Senior College

* Courses are redesigned from existing course technical assistance available through the faculty development office.

* Distance education courses are converted from regular courses or are purchased/leased through PBS.

CHAPTER THREE: EXPANSION PLANS FOR DISTANCE EDUCATION PROGRAMS

95.3% of the colleges surveyed plan to expand their distance education program. A slightly smaller percentage, 94.7%, of those with fewer than 250 students enrolled in distance education plan to expand the program. Every one of the colleges with between 250 and 1,000 students, and with more than 1,000 enrolled, indicated plans to expand its distance education program.

Table #11: Expansion Plans for Established Distance Education Programs, total and break out by number of students enrolled.

Status of Expansion Plans	Total	Fewer than 250	Between 250 and 1,000	More than 1,000
Plan to Expand	95.3%	94.7%	100%	100%
Unsure of Plans to Expand	4.7%	5.3%	0%	0%

All of the colleges in the West and Midwest plan to expand their distance education programs, while 93.3% of those in the South and only 83.3% of those in the Northeast plan to do so.

Table #12: Expansion Plans for Established Distance Education Programs, total and break out by regional location of the college.

Status of Expansion Plans	Total	South	Northeast	Midwest	West
Plan to Expand	95.3%	93.3%	83.3%	100%	100%
Unsure of Plans to Expand	4.7%	6.7%	16.7%	0%	0%

While nearly 100% of the colleges surveyed plan to expand their distance education programs, a slightly higher percentage of senior colleges than of junior colleges indicated that they plan to do so.

Table #13: Expansion Plans for Established Distance Education Programs at Junior Colleges.

Status of Expansion Plans	Percent of Colleges with an established DE program
Plan to Expand	94.7%
Unsure of Plans to Expand	5.3%

Table #14: Expansion Plans for Distance Education Programs at Senior Colleges.

Status of Expansion Plans	Percent of Colleges with an established DE program
Plan to Expand	95.8%
Unsure of Plans to Expand	4.2%

Primary Research asked survey participants to rank the reasons why they planned to expand their distance education programs. The following reasons were listed on the questionnaires for respondents to rank:

To meet greater demand
stay competitive
serve new markets
provide alternatives to traditional student
reduce impact on college facilities
enhance the learning experience
help students become technology literate

Colleges were asked to rank the reasons from 1 to 10, with 1 being very important and 10 being unimportant. The following charts are breakdowns of a ranked listing of the major reasons colleges plan to expand their distance education programs. The reasons of "To Serve New Markets" and "To Meet Greater Demand" scored as the most important reasons for expanding DE programs.

Table #15: SUMMARY CHART: Reasons for Expanding Distance Education Programs.

Reasons for Expanding DE Program	Mean Rank	Median Rank	Minimum	Maximum
To Meet Greater Demand	3.732	3.000	1.000	10.000
To Stay Competitive	4.415	3.000	1.000	10.000
To Serve New Markets	3.650	2.000	1.000	10.000
Provide Alternatives for Traditional Students	4.186	3.000	1.000	10.000
Reduce Impact on College Facilities	6.718	7.000	1.000	10.000
Enhance the Learning Experience	4.051	4.000	1.000	9.000
To Help Students Become Technology Literate	5.342	5.000	1.000	10.000

The mean rank colleges gave "meeting greater demand" as a reason for expanding distance education programs was 3.732; the median rank 3; the minimum rank 1; and the maximum rank 10.

Table #16: Rankings of "to Meet Greater Demand" as a Reason for Expanding Distance Education Programs.

Mean	Median	Minimum	Maximum
3.732	3.000	1.000	10.000

The importance given to "meeting greater demand" decreased as the size of the program increased, suggesting that the smaller programs feel more pressure to grow. The mean rank colleges with fewer than 250 students enrolled in distance education gave "to meet greater demand" as a reason for expanding distance education programs was 3.667; the median rank 3; the minimum rank 1; and the maximum rank 10. The mean rank colleges with between 250 and 1,000 students enrolled in distance education gave was 3.962; the median rank 3; the minimum rank 1; and the maximum rank 9. The mean rank colleges with more than 1,000 students enrolled in distance education gave was 4; the median 2.5; the minimum 1; and the maximum 10.

Table #17: Rankings of "To Meet Greater Demand" as a Reason for Expanding Distance Education Programs, broken out by the number of students enrolled in the program.

Size	Mean	Median	Minimum	Maximum
Fewer Than 250	3.667	3.000	1.000	10.000
Between 250 and 1,000	3.692	3.000	1.000	9.000
More Than 1,000	4.00	2.50	1.00	10.000

Primary Research Group, Inc.   P.O. Box 20853, New York, NY 10023   212/397-5055

The importance of "meeting greater demand" appeared to be similar across the country, with programs in the South placing slightly less emphasis on it than in the other regions. The mean rank colleges in the West gave "to meet greater demand" as a reason for expanding distance education programs was 3.67; the median rank 3; the minimum rank 1; and the maximum rank 10. The mean rank colleges in the South gave was 3.857; the median rank 3; the minimum rank 1; and the maximum rank 10. The mean rank colleges in the Northeast gave was 3.67; the median rank 2.5; the minimum rank 1; and the maximum rank 9. The mean rank colleges in the Midwest gave was 3.667; the median rank 3; the minimum rank 1; and the maximum rank 10.

Table #18: Rankings of "To Meet Greater Demand" as a Reason for Expanding Distance Education Programs, broken out by the regional location of the college.

Region	Mean	Median	Minimum	Maximum
West	3.67	3.00	1.00	10.00
South	3.857	3.000	1.00	10.00
Northeast	3.67	2.50	1.00	9.00
Midwest	3.667	3.000	1.00	10.00

Whether a college is a junior college or a senior college does not appear to be a factor in the ranking of "to meet greater demand" as a reason for expanding distance education programs. The mean rank junior colleges gave "meeting greater demand" was 3.778; the median rank 3; the minimum rank 1; and the maximum rank 9. The mean rank senior colleges gave was 3.696; the median rank 2; the minimum rank 1; and the maximum rank 10.

Table #19: Rankings of "To Meet Greater Demand" as a Reason for Expanding Distance Education Programs, broken out by the level of the college, junior or senior.

Level	Mean	Median	Minimum	Maximum
Junior College	3.778	3.000	1.000	9.000
College	3.696	2.000	1.000	10.000

Primary Research Group, Inc.   P.O. Box 20853, New York, NY 10023   212/397-5055

The mean rank colleges gave "staying competitive" as a reason for expanding distance education programs was 4.145; the median rank 3; the minimum rank 1; and the maximum rank 10.

Table #20: Rankings of "To Stay Competitive" as a Reason for Expanding
Distance Education Programs

Mean	Median	Minimum	Maximum
4.415	3.000	1.000	10.000

Interestingly, staying competitive was more important to programs with between 250 and 1,000 students, while those with fewer than 250 and more than 1,000 were less concerned with doing so. The mean rank colleges with fewer than 250 students enrolled in distance education gave "staying competitive" as a reason for expanding distance education programs was 5.556; the median rank 5; the minimum rank 1; and the maximum rank 10. The mean rank colleges with between 250 and 1,000 students enrolled in distance education gave was 3.145; the median rank 3; the minimum rank 1; and the maximum rank 9. The mean rank colleges with more than 1,000 students enrolled in distance education gave was 4.5; the median rank was 3.5; the minimum rank was 1; and the maximum rank was 10.

Table #21: Rankings of "To Stay Competitive" as a Reason for Expanding Distance Education
Programs, broken out by the number of students enrolled in the program.

Size	Mean	Median	Minimum	Maximum
Fewer Than 250	5.556	5.000	1.000	10.000
Between 250 and 1,000	3.154	3.000	1.000	9.000
More Than 1,000	4.50	3.50	1.00	10.000

Primary Research Group, Inc.   P.O. Box 20853, New York, NY 10023   212/397-5055

The importance of staying competitive does not vary considerably from region to region. The mean rank colleges in the West gave "staying competitive" as a reason for expanding distance education programs was 4.25; the median rank 3.5; the minimum rank 1; and the maximum rank 10. The mean rank colleges in the South gave was 4.57; the median rank 3.5; the minimum rank 1; and the maximum rank 10. The mean rank colleges in the Northeast gave was 4.67; the median rank 5; the minimum rank 1; and the maximum rank 10. The mean rank colleges in the Midwest gave was 4.231; the median rank 3; the minimum rank 1; and the maximum rank 10.

Table #22: Rankings of "To Stay Competitive" as a Reason for Expanding Distance Education Programs, broken out by the regional location of the college.

Region	Mean	Median	Minimum	Maximum
West	4.25	3.50	1.00	10.000
South	4.57	3.50	1.00	10.000
Northeast	4.67	5.00	1.00	10.000
Midwest	4.231	3.000	1.00	10.000

Junior colleges face a little more pressure than senior colleges to use distance learning to match the competition. The mean rank junior colleges gave "staying competitive" as a reason for expanding distance education programs was 3.882; the median rank 3; the minimum rank 1; and the maximum rank 10. The mean rank senior colleges gave was 4.792; the median rank 4; the minimum rank 1; and the maximum rank 10.

Table #23: Rankings of "To Stay Competitive" as a Reason for Expanding Distance Education Programs, broken out by the level of the college, junior or senior.

Status	Mean	Median	Minimum	Maximum
Junior College	3.882	3.000	1.000	10.000
Senior College	4.792	4.000	1.000	10.000

Primary Research Group, Inc.   P.O. Box 20853, New York, NY 10023   212/397-5055

The mean rank colleges gave "serving new markets" as a reason for expanding distance education programs was 3.65; the median rank 2; the minimum rank 1; and the maximum rank 10.

Table #24: Rankings of "To Serve New Markets" as a Reason for Expanding Distance Education Programs.

Mean	Median	Minimum	Maximum
3.650	2.000	1.000	10.000

Not surprisingly, colleges with fewer than 250 students enrolled in distance education are less concerned with serving new markets than are other colleges. The mean rank that colleges with fewer than 250 students enrolled gave "serving new markets" as a reason for expanding distance education programs was 3.833; the median rank 2; the minimum rank 1; and the maximum rank 10. The mean rank for colleges with between 250 and 1,000 students enrolled in distance education was 3.5; the median rank 2.5; the minimum rank 1; and the maximum rank 10. The mean rank for colleges with more than 1,000 students enrolled in distance education was 3.5; the median rank 1.5; the minimum rank 1; and the maximum rank 10.

Table #25: Rankings of "To Serve New Markets" as a Reason for Expanding Distance Education Programs, broken out by the number of students enrolled in the program.

Size	Mean	Median	Minimum	Maximum
Fewer Than 250	3.833	2.000	1.000	10.000
Between 250 and 1,000	3.500	2.500	1.000	10.000
More Than 1,000	3.50	1.50	1.00	10.000

The mean rank colleges gave "providing alternatives to the traditional student" as a reason for expanding distance education programs was 4.186; the median rank 3; the minimum rank 1; and the maximum rank 10.

Table #26: Rankings of "To Provide Alternatives to the Traditional Student" as a Reason for Expanding Distance Education Programs.

Mean	Median	Minimum	Maximum
4.186	3.000	1.000	10.000

The importance of providing alternatives to students varied quite a bit from region to region. The mean rank colleges in the West gave "to provide alternatives to the traditional student" as a reason for expanding distance education programs was 3; the median rank 2; the minimum rank 1; and the maximum rank 8. The mean rank colleges in the South gave was 4.467; the median rank 4; the minimum rank 1; and the maximum rank 10. The mean rank colleges in the Northeast gave was 5.83; the median rank 6.5; the minimum rank 1; and the maximum rank 10. The mean rank colleges in the Midwest gave was 3.923; the median rank 2; the minimum rank 1; and the maximum rank 10.

Table #27: Rankings of "To Provide Alternatives To The Traditional Student" as a Reason for Expanding Distance Education Programs, broken out by the regional location of the college.

Region	Mean	Median	Minimum	Maximum
West	3.000	2.000	1.000	8.000
South	4.467	4.000	1.000	10.000
Northeast	5.83	6.50	1.00	10.000
Midwest	3.923	2.000	1.000	10.000

Overall, senior colleges were more concerned with the options of traditional students while the junior colleges tended to see distance learning as a means to serve new or difficult to reach populations. The mean rank junior colleges gave "providing alternatives to the traditional student" as a reason for expanding distance education programs was 4.579; the median rank 3; the minimum rank 1; and the maximum rank 10. The mean rank senior colleges gave was 3.975; the median rank 2.5; the minimum rank 1; and the maximum rank 10. The above data are captured in table #28 on the following page.

Table #28: Rankings of "To Provide Alternatives To The Traditional Student" as a Reason for Expanding Distance Education Programs, broken out by the level of the college, junior or senior.

Status	Mean	Median	Minimum	Maximum
Junior College	4.579	3.000	1.000	10.000
Senior College	3.875	2.500	1.000	10.000

In general, colleges were not motivated to develop distance learning programs in order to reduce the impact of enrollment increases on college facilities or infrastructure, although this may become a more important reason in the near future. Colleges in the Northeast were a bit more concerned than other colleges with this reason. The mean rank colleges gave for this reason was 6.718; the median 7.000; the minimum 1.000; and the maximum 10.000.

Table #29: Rankings of "To Reduce the Impact on College Facilities" as a Reason for Expanding Distance Education Programs.

Mean	Median	Minimum	Maximum
6.718	7.000	1.000	10.000

Junior colleges gave "to reduce the impact on college facilities" as a reason to expand distance education programs a mean rank of 6.222; a median of 5.500; a minimum of 1.000; and a maximum of 10.000. Ranks given by senior colleges were even lower, a mean of 7.143; a median of 8.000; a minimum of 1.000; and a maximum of 10.000.

Table #30: Rankings of "To Reduce the Impact on College Facilities" as a Reason for Expanding Distance Education Programs, broken out by the level of the college, junior or senior.

Status	Mean	Median	Minimum	Maximum
Junior College	6.222	5.500	1.000	10.000
College	7.143	8.000	1.000	10.000

The distribution by number of students in the program was pretty much even. The mean rank colleges with fewer than 250 students enrolled in distance education gave "reducing the impact on colleges facilities" as a reason for expanding distance education was 6.471; the median rank 7; the minimum rank 1; and the maximum rank 10. The mean rank colleges with between 250 and 1,000 students enrolled in distance education was 6.667; the median rank 7; the minimum rank 3; and the maximum rank 10. The mean rank colleges with more than 1,000 students enrolled in distance education gave was 6.25; the median rank 6.5; the minimum rank 3; and the maximum rank 9.

Table #31: Rankings of "To Reduce The Impact On College Facilities" as a Reason for Expanding Distance Education Programs, broken out by the number of students enrolled in the program.

Size	Mean	Median	Minimum	Maximum
Fewer Than 250	6.471	7.000	1.000	10.000
Between 250 and 1,000	6.667	7.000	3.000	10.000
More Than 1,000	6.25	6.50	3.000	9.000

The mean rank colleges in the West gave "reducing the impact on college facilities" as a reason for expanding distance education programs was 6.667; the median rank 7; the minimum rank 4; and the maximum rank 9. The mean rank colleges in the South gave was 6.667; the median rank 7.5; the minimum rank 1; and the maximum rank 10. The mean rank colleges in the Northeast gave was 5; the median rank 5; the minimum rank 1; and the maximum rank 9. The mean rank in the Midwest was 7.667; the median rank 8.5; the minimum rank 4; and the maximum rank 10. The above data are shown in table #32 on the following page.

Table #32: Rankings of "To Reduce The Impact On College Facilities" as a Reason for Expanding Distance Education Programs, broken out by regional location of the college.

Region	Mean	Median	Minimum	Maximum
West	6.667	7.000	4.000	9.000
South	6.667	7.500	1.000	10.000
Northeast	5.00	5.00	1.00	9.00
Midwest	7.667	8.500	4.000	10.000

The mean rank colleges gave "enhancing the learning experience" as a reason for expanding distance education programs was 4.051; the median rank 4; the minimum rank 1; and the maximum rank 9.

Table #33: Rankings of "To Enhance The Learning Experience" as a Reason for Expanding Distance Education Programs.

Mean	Median	Minimum	Maximum
4.051	4.000	1.000	9.000

In general, as shown in table #34 on the following page, colleges with more than 1,000 students enrolled in higher education gave a higher rank to "to enhance the learning experience" than other colleges. The mean rank colleges with fewer than 250 students enrolled in distance education gave "enhancing the learning experience" as a reason for expanding distance education programs was 4.222; the median rank 3.5; the minimum rank 1; and the maximum rank 9. The mean rank colleges with between 250 and 1,000 students enrolled in distance education gave was 4.75; the median rank 4.5; the minimum rank 1; and the maximum rank 8. The mean rank colleges with more than 1,000 students enrolled in distance education gave was 3; the median 2.5; the minimum 1; and the maximum 6.

Table #34: Rankings of "To Enhance The Learning Experience" as a Reason for Expanding Distance Education Programs, broken out by the number of students enrolled in the program.

Size	Mean	Median	Minimum	Maximum
Fewer Than 250	4.222	3.500	1.000	9.000
Between 250 and 1,000	4.750	4.500	1.000	8.000
More Than 1,000	3.000	2.500	1.000	6.000

The importance given to "enhancing higher education" varied somewhat in each of the regions, with the South giving the highest ranking and the West giving the lowest. The mean rank colleges in the West gave "to enhance the learning experience" as a reason for expanding distance education programs was 5; the median 5; the minimum 1; and the maximum 9. The mean rank colleges in the South gave was 3.308; the median 3; the minimum 1; and the maximum 6. The mean rank colleges in the Northeast gave was 4.2; the median 4; the minimum 1; and the maximum 7. The mean rank colleges in the Midwest gave was 4.154; the median 5; the minimum 1; and the maximum 8.

Table #35: Rankings of "To Enhance The Learning Experience" as a Reason for Expanding Distance Education Programs, broken out by the regional location of the college.

Region	Mean	Median	Minimum	Maximum
West	5.000	5.000	1.000	9.000
South	3.308	3.000	1.000	6.000
Northeast	4.200	4.000	1.000	7.000
Midwest	4.154	5.000	1.000	8.000

The mean rank junior colleges gave "enhancing the learning experience" as a reason for expanding distance education programs was 4.375; the median 4.5; the minimum 1; and the maximum 8. The mean rank senior colleges gave was 3.826; the median 4; the minimum 1; and the maximum 9.

Table #36: Rankings of "To Enhance The Learning Experience" as a Reason for Expanding Distance Education Programs, broken out by the level of the college, junior or senior.

Status	Mean	Median	Minimum	Maximum
Junior College	4.375	4.500	1.000	8.000
Senior College	3.826	4.000	1.000	9.000

The mean rank colleges gave "helping students become technology literate" as a reason for expanding distance education programs was 5.342; the median 5; the minimum 1; and the maximum 10.

Table #37: Rankings of "To Help Students Become Technology Literate" as a Reason for Expanding Distance Education Programs.

Mean	Median	Minimum	Maximum
5.342	5.000	1.000	10.000

As indicated in table #38 on the following page, the importance given to "helping students become technology literate" increased with the number of students enrolled in the program. The mean rank colleges with fewer than 250 students enrolled in DE gave "helping students become technology literate" as a reason for expanding distance education programs was 6.118; the median 6; the minimum 2; and the maximum 10. The mean rank colleges with between 250 and 1,000 students enrolled in distance education gave was 5.25; the median 5; the minimum 3; and the maximum 8. The mean rank colleges with more than 1,000 students enrolled in distance education gave was 4.5; the median 4.5; the minimum 3; and the maximum 6.

Table #38: Rankings of "To Help Students Become Technology Literate" as a Reason for Expanding Distance Education Programs, broken out by the number of students enrolled in the program.

Size	Mean	Median	Minimum	Maximum
Fewer Than 250	6.118	6.000	2.000	10.000
Between 250 and 1,000	5.250	5.000	3.000	8.000
More Than 1,000	4.500	4.500	3.000	6.000

The colleges in the West were somewhat less concerned with "helping students become technology literate" than those in the other regions. The mean rank colleges in the West gave "helping students become technology literate" as a reason for expanding distance education programs was 6.5; the median 6.5; the minimum 3; and the maximum 10. The mean rank colleges in the South gave was 5.154; the median 5; the minimum 1; and the maximum 10. The mean rank colleges in the Northeast gave was 5; the median 5; the minimum 3; and the maximum 7. The mean rank colleges in the Midwest gave was 4.917; the median 5; the minimum 2; and the maximum 8.

Table #39: Rankings of "To Help Students Become Technology Literate" as a Reason for Expanding Distance Education Programs, broken out by regional location of the college.

Region	Mean	Median	Minimum	Maximum
West	6.500	6.500	3.000	10.000
South	5.154	5.000	1.000	10.000
Northeast	5.000	5.000	3.000	7.000
Midwest	4.917	5.000	2.000	8.000

CHAPTER FOUR: FULL DEGREE PROGRAMS THROUGH DISTANCE EDUCATION

44.2% of colleges with an established distance education program offer a full degree program through distance education. Not surprisingly, the highest concentration of full degree programs is in those distance education programs with more than 1,000 students. 36.8% of colleges with less than 250 students offer a full degree program through distance education, while only 35.7% of colleges with between 250 and 1,000 students do the same. In contrast, 75% of colleges with more than 1,000 students offer a full degree program through distance education.

Table #40: Percentage of Colleges That Offer A Full Degree Program Through Distance Education, total and break out by the number of students enrolled in the program.

Degree Program Status	Total	Less Than 250	Between 250 and 1,000	More than 1,000
Offer Full Degree Program	44.2%	36.8%	35.7%	75%
Do Not Offer Full Degree Program	55.8%	63.2%	64.3%	25%

The percentage of colleges that offer a full degree program through distance education differs slightly from region to region, with the highest percentage in the Northeast and the lowest in the West. 46.7% of colleges located in the South offer a full degree program through distance education, as do 50% of colleges located in the Northeast. 46.2% of colleges located in the Midwest and only 33.3% of colleges located in the West offer a full degree program through distance education.

Table #41: Percentage of Colleges That Offer A Full Degree Program Through Distance Education, total and break out by the regional location of the school.

Degree Program Status	Total	South	Northeast	Midwest	West
Offer Full Degree Program	44.2%	46.7%	50%	46.2%	33.3%
Do Not Offer Full Degree Program	55.8%	53.3%	50%	53.8%	66.7%

Primary Research Group, Inc. P.O. Box 20853, New York. NY 10023 212/397-5055

Only 21% of junior colleges offer a full degree program through distance education, while 62.5% of senior colleges do the same.

Table #42: Percentage of Junior Colleges That Offer A Full Degree Program Through Distance Education.

Degree Program Status	Percent of Colleges
Offer Full Degree Program	21%
Do Not Offer Full Degree Program	79%

Table #43: Percentage of Senior Colleges That Offer A Full Degree Program Through Distance Education.

Degree Program Status	Percent of Colleges
Offer Full Degree Program	62.5%
Do Not Offer Full Degree Program	37.5%

Only 44% of the colleges in the sample offered full degree programs through distance education. A list of the degrees offered by some of the colleges in the sample that listed them appears below:

* Degrees offered: An MBA and an MA in management
    -- University

* Offers 27 degrees. B.A; B.S; M.S; M.A; M.B.A
    -- University with more than 15,000 students

* Offers these degrees: business management, marketing, automotive management, accounting, agribusiness marketing, business computer application, legal assisting, travel management, medical office assistant, pharmacy assistant, legal secretary, medical secretary.
    -- Senior College

* Degrees offered: MS in Education, MS in Organization/Management
        -- Graduate School

* Degrees offered: MBA, BA.
        -- Senior College with fewer than 5,000 students

* Degrees offered: MS Social Work, MS Communications, Phd Education, MS Information
Science, MS Engineering Management.
        -- University with more than 15,000 students

* Offers a degree in Graphics Communication.
        -- Junior College with between 5,000 and 15,000 students

* Degrees offered: MS ECE, MS Computer Science.
        -- University with more than 15,000 students

* Degrees offered: MA in Human Development; BA in Human Development (final year).
        -- Senior College with fewer than 5,000 students

* Degrees offered: Master of Arts, General Theological Studies Pilot Program.
    -- Seminary

* Degrees offered: RN to BSN; RT to RMI; BS in Business; MSN in Education; MSN in
Administration; MSN in Family Nurse Practitioner; MS in Health Services Management; Family
Nurse Practitioner Post Master's Certificate.
    -- Senior College with fewer than 5,000 students

* Degrees offered: AA degree.
        -- Senior College with between 5,000 and 15,000 students

* Degrees offered: Bachelor of General Studies
        -- Senior College with fewer than 5,000 students

* Degrees offered: BA Information Systems; BS Computer Science; MS Engineering Technology;
MS Information Systems and 6 graduate certificates.
    -- Junior College with between 5,000 and 15,000 students

* Degrees offered: Associate (2 year degrees) Dental Hygiene, AAB, Educational Interpreter
Technician, Accounting, Supervising Management.
    --Senior College with more than 15,000 students

* Degrees offered: Master of Science in Education

* Degrees offered: Master of Science in Health Administration.

* Degrees offered: Business Administration
  -- University with between 5,000 and 15,000 students

* Degrees offered: AA; AAS; BA; BEd; MEd; certificates.

CHAPTER FIVE: COURSES AND ENROLLMENT

The mean number of distance education courses offered by the schools surveyed was 35.07; the median number, 22. The minimum number of courses offered was 2; the maximum 200.

Table #44: The Number Of Distance Education Courses Offered In Colleges With Established DE Programs.

Mean	Median	Minimum	Maximum
35.07	22.00	2	200

The mean number of classes offered in schools with fewer than 250 students enrolled in distance education was 18.74; the median 15; the minimum 4; and the maximum 75. There was only a slight increase in the number of classes offered in schools with between 250 and 1,000 students, the mean was 31.29; the median 30; the minimum 12; and the maximum 80.

A more substantial increase occurred in the next group--schools with more than 1,000 students--the mean was 124; the median 130; the minimum, 36, and the maximum, 200.

Table #45: The Number of Distance Education Courses Offered, broken out by the number of students enrolled in the program.

Number of Students Enrolled in DE Courses	Mean Number of Courses	Median	Minimum	Maximum
Fewer Than 250	18.74	15.00	4.00	75.00
Between 250 and 1,000	31.29	30.00	12.00	80.00
More Than 1,000	124.00	130.00	36.00	200.0

In general, colleges in the Midwest offered more distance education courses, per college, than in any other region. Colleges in the West offered the least. The mean number of distance education courses offered at each college in the West was 22.67; the median 20.00; the minimum 8.00; the maximum 90.00. The mean number at each college in the South was 31.9; the median 25.0; the minimum 3.00; and the maximum 125.00. The mean number at each college in the Northeast was 33.8; the median 22.0; the minimum 2.00; the maximum 200.00. The mean number at each college in the Midwest was 44.0; the median 22.0; the minimum 2.00; and the maximum 200.00.

Table #46: The Number of Distance Education Courses Offered, broken out by the regional location of the program.

Status	Mean	Median	Minimum	Maximum
West	22.67	20.00	8.00	90.00
South	31.9	25.0	3.00	125.00
Northeast	33.8	22.0	2.00	200.00
Midwest	44.4	22.0	2.00	200.00

The difference between the number of distance education courses offered by junior colleges and by 4-year colleges is surprising. Despite the usually overall smaller scale of junior colleges the number is quite close. Colleges offer only 8.9 more courses, on average, than junior colleges.

The mean number for junior colleges is 30.2; the median 20; the minimum 3; the maximum 200. The mean number for colleges is 38.92; the median 24.5; the minimum 2; the maximum 170.

Table #47: The Number of Distance Education Courses Offered, broken out by the level of the college, junior or senior.

Status	Mean	Median	Minimum	Maximum
Junior Colleges	30.2	20.0	3.0	200.0
Senior Colleges	38.92	24.50	2.0	170.0

The number of students per college enrolled in distance education courses varies greatly, with one school testing the waters on distance education in a pilot program with only 5 students, while another enrolls 12,000 students. The mean number is 821; the median, 233.

Table #48: The Mean and Median Number Of Students Per College Program Enrolled in Distance Education Courses.

Mean	Median	Minimum	Maximum
821	233	5	12,000

In general, more students were enrolled in distance education, per college program, in the South than in any other region.

Table #49: The Number of Students Per College Program Enrolled In Distance Education Courses, broken out by the regional location of the college.

Status	Mean	Median	Minimum	Maximum
West	619	240	55	2700
South	1172	203	5	12000
Northeast	366	295	100	775
Midwcst	723	215	18	6000

The maximum number of students enrolled in distance education at a junior college, 6,000, was exactly half the maximum number of students enrolled in DE at a senior college, 12,000. For junior colleges the mean number was 674; the median 237; and the minimum 27. For senior colleges the mean number was 942; the median 222; and the minimum 5. The above data are captured in table #50 on the following page.

Table #50: The Number of Students Per College Program Enrolled In Distance Education Courses, broken out by the level of the college, junior or senior.

Status	Mean	Median	Minimum	Maximum
Junior Colleges	674	237	27	6000
Senior Colleges	942	222	5	12000

The distance learning enrollment population is more volatile than the traditional student population at most institutions. The median number of students was 233 in all programs, while the median number of students in the past semester was 172. The mean number was even more volatile; the annual average number of students enrolled in DE programs in the survey was 821, while the mean for the past semester was only 428, suggesting strong growth, or a volatile student population that eases into and exits from DE programs relatively quickly.

The mean number of students per college program who took a distance learning class last semester was 428; the median 172; the minimum 0; the maximum 4,200. The "last semester" would be the Spring semester of 1997.

Table #51: The Mean and Median Number Of Students Per College Program Enrolled in Distance Education Courses Last Semester.

Mean	Median	Minimum	Maximum
428	172	0	4200

The mean number of students that took a distance education course, last semester, at a college with fewer than 250 student enrolled in DE was 150.3; the median 69.0; the minimum 0; the maximum 990. The mean number of students at a college with between 250 and 1,000 students enrolled in DE was 399.0; the median 400.0; the minimum 55.0; and the maximum 680.0. The mean number of students at a college with more than 1,000 students enrolled in DE was 2,922.0; the median 3,500.0; the minimum 1,065.0; and the maximum 4,200. The above data are shown in table #52 on the following page.

Table #52: The Number Of Students Per College Program Enrolled In Distance Education Courses Last Semester, broken out by the number of students enrolled in the program.

Status	Mean	Median	Minimum	Maximum
Fewer Than 250	150.3	69.0	0.0	990.0
Between 250 and 1,000	399.0	400.0	55.0	680.0
More Than 1,000	2922.0	3500.0	1065.0	4200.0

Per program, colleges in the West enrolled more students in distance education last semester than did colleges in any other region, across the board. In the West, the mean number of students was 746; the median 200; the minimum 50; and the maximum 3,500. In general, colleges in the South, the Northeast, and the Midwest enrolled far fewer students, and in some cases enrolled none at all.

Table #53: The Number of Students Per College Program Enrolled in Distance Education Courses Semester, broken out by the regional location of the college.

Status	Mean	Median	Minimum	Maximum
West	746	200	50	3500
South	486	144	0	4200
Northeast	106.8	55.0	0.0	255
Midwest	233.4	120.0	0.0	680

Primary Research Group, Inc.   P.O. Box 20853, New York, NY 10023   212/397-5055

The mean number of students who took a distance learning class through a junior college program, last semester was 301.8; the median 197; the minimum 0; and the maximum 1,065. The mean number for senior colleges was 530; the median 135; the minimum 0; the maximum 4,200.

Table #54: The Number Of Students Per College Program Enrolled in Distance Education Courses Last Semester, broken out by the level of the college, junior or senior.

Status	Mean	Median	Minimum	Maximum
Junior Colleges	301.8	197.0	0.0	1065.0
Senior Colleges	530	135	0.0	4200.0

STUDENT DEMOGRAPHICS

83.3% of colleges with distance education programs collect demographic information about the kinds of students that take distance learning classes.

Table #55: Percentage of Colleges With Distance Education Programs That Collect Demographic Information.

Demographic Collection Status	Percent of Colleges
Collect Demographic Information	83.3%
Do Not Collect Demographic Information	16.7%

We asked survey participants to compare the demographics of their distance learning students with that of their students taking traditional "in-classroom" courses. We had hoped to obtain quantitative information that would enable us to contrast the two populations. We found that most schools did not have such information at their fingertips, but only collected information in a relatively informal way. They did have a general feel for the questions, if not the specific data that we were seeking. About a quarter of the sample provided specific quantitative information but we have decided against presenting it, since the sample is very small and skewed to very large and very small programs.

The subjective impressions of some of the survey participants, which follow, are instructive nonetheless.

* In general, distance learning students are older than other students.

* Demographic differences: We aim to serve adult students -thus, older, more women.
     -- Senior College

* There are no demographic differences between distance learning students and students enrolled in more traditional courses of study.
     -- Junior College

* Demographic differences include a more Native Americans in the DE program. The average age of DE students is 34, as compared to 26 for traditional.
     -- University with more than 15,000 students

* Demographic differences: distance learning students are mostly working adults, over 22.
     -- Senior College

* Demographic differences: there are a greater proportion of males.
   -- Junior College with between 5,000 and 15,000 students

* Demographic differences: more working, with families.
     -- Senior College with fewer than 5,000 students

* Demographic differences: older students and working students are in distance ed.
     -- University with more than 15,000 students

* DE students are very similar to campus based population (particularly part-time evening). Average age is 30, taking at least 6 credits.
     -- Junior College with more than 15,000 students

* There are no major demographic differences between DE students and students enrolled in more traditional courses of study. Traditional aged students choose distance learning to add credit hours to an on-campus schedule of classes. Older than average students choose for convenience. Largest percentage are female, ages 25 to 35.
     -- University with between 5,000 and 15,000 students

* Distance learning students are usually 5 to 10 years older than students in more traditional courses of study.
     -- University with more than 15,000 students

* Average age of on-line students is a bit older--say 40, rather than 35. On campus students may also enroll for MA in Counseling and for teacher certification, programs not available on-line.
     -- Senior College with fewer than 5,000 students

Primary Research Group, Inc.   P.O. Box 20853, New York, NY 10023   212/397-5055

* There are more single parents and more disabled students in distance learning programs, than in traditional programs.
     -- Junior College with more than 15,000 students

* Distance education students are, on the average, older than students in more traditional programs of study. The average age for DE students is 39. The average on-campus age is 39.
     -- University

* There are more older people, career people, and people who are "testing the waters" of attending seminary in distance education.
     -- Seminary

* Distance Education students are traditionally 5-10 years older, married, work full-time, and have children.
     -- Senior College with fewer than 5,000 students

* Distance education students are very similar to those on-campus in similar courses.
     -- University with between 5,000 and 15,000 students

* Distance education students tend to be older; all are working and/or have families.
     -- Senior College with between 5,000 and 15,000 students

* Distance education students all have full-time responsibilities off-campus.
   -- Senior College with fewer than 5,000 students

* Demographically, distance education students are older, and more are part time.
     -- Junior College with between 5,000 and 15,000 students

* Adult, placebound students take distance education courses.
     -- Senior College with between 5,000 and 15,000 students

* Distance education students are generally older.
     -- Senior College with more than 15,000 students

* All distance education students are experienced teachers in New England and New York.

* Distance education students are older, employed full time, more often motivated to get degree for career advancement/change.
     -- University with more than 15,000 students

* Demographic differences: usually older; greater percentage of women; more natives Americans.

Primary Research Group, Inc.   P.O. Box 20853, New York, NY 10023   212/397-5055

CHAPTER SIX: MARKETING AND SELLING DISTANCE EDUCATION

23.3% of colleges with distance education programs market the distance education courses only to their own students.

Table #56: Percentage of Colleges that Market Distance Education Courses
Only To Their Own Students

Marketing Status	Percentage of Colleges in Sample
Market Only To Their Own Students	23.3%
Market Outside of Their Own Students	76.7%

Table #57: Percentage of Colleges That Market Distance Education Courses Only To Their Own Students, total and break out by the number of students enrolled in the program.

Marketing Status	Total	Fewer than 250	Between 250 and 1,000	More than 1,000
Market Only To Their Own Students	23.3%	26.3%	7.1%	50%
Market Outside of Their Own Students	76.7%	73.7%	92.9%	50%

Table #58: Percentage of Colleges That Market Distance Education Courses Only To Their Own Students, total and break out by the regional location of the college.

Marketing Status	Total	South	Northeast	Midwest	West
Market Only To Their Own Students	23.3%	13.3%	16.7%	38.5%	22.2%
Market Outside of Their Own Students	76.7%	86.7%	83.3%	61.5%	77.8%

26.3% of junior colleges, and 20.8% of senior colleges, market distance education courses just to their own students.

Table #59: Percentage of Junior Colleges That Market Distance Education Courses Only To Their Own Students.

Marketing Status	Percent of Colleges
Market Only To Their Own Students	26.3%
Market Outside of Their Own Students	73.7%

Table #60: Percentage of Senior Colleges That Market Distance Education Courses Only To Their Own Students.

Marketing Status	Percent of Colleges
Market Only To Their Own Students	20.8%
Market Outside of Their Own Students	79.2%

Larger and more prominent distance education programs are trying to cash in on the rapid development of distance learning, and the relative absence of private sector publishers, by selling courses and program materials to other programs, and to individuals and institutions in foreign countries.

As shown in table #61 on the following page, 23.3% of colleges attempt to sell or license distance learning services to other organizations.

10.5% of colleges with fewer than 250 students, 28.6% of colleges with between 250 and 1,000 students, and 50% of colleges with more than 1,000 students attempt to sell or license DE services to other organizations.

59

Table #61: Percentage of Colleges That Attempt to Sell or License Distance Education Services to Other Organizations, total and break out by number of students enrolled in the program.

Selling And Licensing Status	Total	Less than 250	Between 250 and 1,000	More than 250
Attempt to Sell And License To Other Organizations	23.3%	10.5%	28.6%	10.5%
Service Restricted To Their Own Institution	76.7%	89.5%	71.4%	89.5%

The percentage of colleges that attempt to sell or license distance learning services to other organizations differs quite a bit from region to region. 40% of colleges located in the South, 16.7% of colleges located in the Northeast, 23% of colleges located in the Midwest, and none of the colleges located in the West attempt to sell or license distance learning services to other organizations.

Table #62: Percentage of Colleges That Attempt to Sell or License Distance Education Services to Other Organizations, total and break out by regional location of college.

Selling And Licensing Status	Total	South	Northeast	Midwest	West
Attempt to Sell And License To Other Organizations	23.3%	40%	16.7%	23.0%	0%
Service Restricted To Their Own Institution	76.7%	60%	83.3%	77.0%	100%

Only 21% of junior colleges attempt to sell or license DE services to other organizations, while 25% of senior colleges do the same.

Table #63: Percentage of Junior Colleges That Attempt to Sell or License Distance Education Services to Other Organizations.

Selling And Licensing Status	Percent of Colleges
Attempt to Sell And License To Other Organizations	21%
Service Restricted To Their Own Institution	79%

Table #64: Percentage of Senior Colleges That Attempt to Sell or License Distance Education Services to Other Organizations.

Selling And Licensing Status	Percent of Colleges
Attempt to Sell And License To Other Organizations	25%
Service Restricted To Their Own Institution	75%

As indicated in table #65 on the following page, 4.7% of the total sample of colleges, all of which had fewer than 250 students enrolled in distance education, have sold a DE course to an organization in a developing country.

Table #65: Percentage of Colleges That Have Sold A Distance Education Course to an Organization in a Developing Country, total and break out by number of students enrolled in the program.

Status	Total	Less than 250	Between 250 and 1,000	More than 1,000
Sold Distance Learning Course to an Organization in a Developing Country	4.7%	5.3%	0.0%	0.0%
Has Not Sold A Distance Learning Course to an Organization in a Developing Country	95.3%	94.7%	100.0%	100.0%

All of the colleges that have sold a distance education course to an organization in a developing country were located either in South or in the Northeast. 6.7% of colleges in the South have done so, as have 16.7% of colleges in the Northeast.

Table #66: Percentage of Colleges That Have Sold A Distance Education Course to an Organization in a Developing Country, total and break out by regional location of the college.

Status	Total	South	Northeast	Mid-west	West
Sold Distance Learning Course to an Organization in a Developing Country	4.7%	6.7%	16.7%	0.0%	0.0%
Has Not Sold A Distance Learning Course to an Organization in a Developing Country	95.3%	93.3%	83.3%	100.0%	100.0%

Primary Research Group, Inc.   P.O. Box 20853, New York, NY 10023   212/397-5055

Perhaps not surprising, none of the junior colleges has sold a distance learning course to an organization in a developing country. Only 8.3% of the senior colleges have done so.

Table #67: Percentage of Junior Colleges That Have Sold A Distance Education Course to an Organization in a Developing Country.

Status	Percent of Colleges
Sold Distance Learning Course to an Organization in a Developing Country	0%
Has Not Sold A Distance Learning Course to an Organization in a Developing Country	100%

Table #68: Percentage of Senior Colleges That Have Sold A Distance Education Course to an Organization in a Developing Country.

Status	Percent of Colleges
Sold Distance Learning Course to an Organization in a Developing Country	8.3%
Has Not Sold A Distance Learning Course to an Organization in a Developing Country	91.7%

It appears that the only foreign countries to which colleges have sold distance education courses are the aforementioned developing countries. The percentages are the same across the board.

Table #69: Percentage of Colleges That Have Sold A Distance Education Course to an Organization in a Foreign Country, total and break out by the number of students enrolled in the program.

Status	Total	Less than 250	Between 250 and 1,000	More than 250
Sold Distance Learning Course to an Organization in a Developing Country	4.7%	5.3%	0.0%	0.0%
Has Not Sold A Distance Learning Course to an Organization in a Developing Country	95.3%	94.7%	100.0%	100.0%

Table #70: Percentage of Colleges That Have Sold A Distance Education Course to an Organization in a Foreign Country, total and break out by regional location of the college.

Status	Total	South	Northeast	Midwest	West
Sold Distance Learning Course to an Organization in a Developing Country	4.7%	6.7%	16.7%	0.0%	0.0%
Has Not Sold A Distance Learning Course to an Organization in a Developing Country	95.3%	93.3%	83.3%	100.0%	100.0%

Primary Research Group, Inc.   P.O. Box 20853, New York, NY 10023   212/397-5055

Table #71: Percentage of Junior Colleges That Have Sold A Distance Education Course to an Organization in a Foreign Country.

Status	Percent of Colleges
Sold Distance Learning Course to an Organization in a Developing Country	0%
Has Not Sold A Distance Learning Course to an Organization in a Developing Country	100%

Table #72: Percentage of Senior Colleges That Have Sold A Distance Learning Course to an Organization in a Foreign Country.

Status	Percent of Colleges
Sold Distance Learning Course to an Organization in a Developing Country	8.3%
Has Not Sold A Distance Learning Course to an Organization in a Developing Country	100%

Many distance learning programs are started "by the seat of the pants" and then grow as administrators gradually "feel their way" and assess the market in a relatively ad hoc way. While the seat of the pants, feel your way approach to distance learning marketing may be perfectly suitable for a small college groping for its role in the developing distance learning market, its limitations will hold back colleges that exist amongst, or can create, significant distance learning demand, and substantial programs. Currently, only about half of all administrators make any attempt to investigate or verify market dimensions.

51.2% of colleges with established distance education programs have made an effort to assess the market demand for DE courses, as shown in table #73 on the following page.

Table #73: Percentage of Colleges That Make An Effort To Assess Market Demand For Distance Education Courses.

Status	Percent of Colleges
Make An Effort To Assess Market Demand	51.2%
Do Not Make An Effort To Assess Market Demand	48.8%

The percentage of junior colleges that made an effort to assess market demand for distance education courses was significantly smaller than that of senior colleges. 36.8% of junior colleges did so, as compared with 62.5% of senior colleges.

Table #74: The Percentage of Junior and Senior Colleges That Make An Effort To Assess Market Demand for Distance Education Courses.

Status	Junior Colleges	Colleges
Make An Effort To Asses Market Demand	36.8%	62.5%
Do Not Make An Effort To Asses Market Demand	63.2%	37.5%

The range of the amount colleges spent to market and advertise their distance education courses within the past year was great. The minimum amount was nothing, the maximum amount was $137,500. The mean was $17,308.00; the median $5000.00.

Table #75: The Amount Colleges Spent To Market And Advertise Distance Education Courses In The Past Year.

Mean	Median	Minimum	Maximum
$17,308.00	$5,000.00	$0.00	$137,500

Primary Research Group, Inc.   P.O. Box 20853, New York, NY 10023   212/397-5055

Not surprisingly, the amount a college spent to market and advertise its distance education courses in the past year, increased as the number of students enrolled in its distance education program increased. The mean amount for colleges with fewer than 250 students enrolled in distance education was $4,536; the median $1,000; the minimum $0.00; the maximum $15,000. The mean amount for colleges with between 250 and 1,000 students was $19,389; the median $5,000; the minimum $0.00; the maximum $137,500. The mean amount for colleges with more than 1,000 students was $27,770; the median $10,000; the minimum $3,310; the maximum $70,000.

Table #76: The Amount Colleges Spent To Market And Advertise Distance Education Courses In The Past Year, broken out by the number of students enrolled in the program.

Status	Mean	Median	Minimum	Maximum
Fewer Than 250	$4,536.00	$1000.00	$0.00	$15,000.00
Between 250 and 1,000	$19,389.00	$5000.00	$0.00	$137,500.00
More Than 1,000	$27,770.00	$10,000.00	$3,310.00	$70,000.00

Table #77: The Amount Colleges Spent to Market and Advertise Distance Education Courses In The Past Year, broken out by the regional location of the college.

Status	Mean	Median	Minimum	Maximum
West	$6,985.00	$6,800.00	$0.00	$15,000.00
South	$11,811.00	$5,000.00	$0.00	$70,000.00
Northeast	$93,750.00	$93,750.00	$50,000.00	$137,500.00
Midwest	$12,125.00	$2500.00	$500.00	$75,000.00

Last year senior colleges spent a great amount more than junior colleges to market and advertise their distance education courses. The mean amount for junior colleges was $3,973; the median $3,310; the minimum $0.00; the maximum $9,500. The mean amount for colleges was $22,494; the median $5,800; the minimum $0.00; the maximum $137,500.

Table #78: The Amount Colleges Spent to Market and Advertise Distance Education Courses In The Past Year, broken out by the level of The college, junior or senior.

Status	Mean	Median	Minimum	Maximum
Junior Colleges	$3,973.00	$3,310.00	$0.00	$9,500.00
Senior Colleges	$22,494.00	$5,800.00	$0.00	$137,500.00

MARKETING RESPONSIBILITY

No single department dominated the responsibility for marketing college distance education classes. Participants were asked to name the department that had this responsibility in their institution. The responses of those institutions responding to this question are listed below:

* The chief of distance learning operations is responsible for marketing DE courses.
    -- Junior College

* The marketing coordinator is responsible for markcting DE courses.
    -- University with more than 15 thousand students

* Admissions is responsible for markcting DE courses.
    -- Senior College

* Continuing education is responsible for marketing distancc education courses.
    -- University with fewer than 5,000 students

* The Director of Communications is responsible for marketing DE courses.
    -- Graduate School

* The instructional division is responsible for marketing distance education courses.
    -- Junior College with fewer than 5,000 students

* The Office of Instruction and the Public Relations Office are responsible for marketing distance education courses.
    -- Senior College with between 5,000 and 15,000 students

* The community relations office is responsible for marketing distance education courses.
    -- Junior College with between 5,000 and 15,000 students

* Regional programs are responsible for marketing distance education courses.
  -- Senior College with fewer than 5,000 students

* The Division Marketing Department is responsible for marketing DE courses.
  -- University with more than 15,000 students

* The media/distance ed. program is responsible for marketing distance education courses.
    -- Senior College with more than 15,000 thousand students

* The public relations officer is responsible for marketing distance education courses.
    -- Junior College with between 5,000 and 15,000 students

* The SUNY Learning Network and Local Public Information Office is responsible for marketing distance education courses.
    -- Junior College with between 5,000 and 15,000 students

* The coordinator of the Office for Extended Learning is responsible for marketing distance education courses.
    -- Junior College with more than 15, 000 students

* The academic divisions are responsible for marketing distance education courses.
    -- Junior College with more than 15,000 students

* The continuing education office is responsible for marketing distance education courses.
    -- University with between 5,000 and 15,000 students

* The Off-Campus Studies Department is responsible for marketing distance education courses.
    -- University with more than 15,000 students

* Deans and PR are responsible for marketing distance education courses.
    -- Junior College with between 5,000 and 15,000 students

* Admissions and Recruiting, Public Relations, and the Distance Learning Coordinator are responsible for marketing distance education courses.
    -- Senior College with fewer than 5,000 students

* The college Publication Department is responsible for marketing distance education courses.
    -- Junior College with more than 15,000 students

* The school of business associate dean and faculty is responsible for marketing distance education courses.
    -- University

* The Director of College Relations is responsible for marketing distance education courses.
    -- Senior College with fewer than 5,000 students

* Graduate Studies is responsible for marketing distance education courses.
    -- Senior College with fewer than 5,000 students

* The Seminary Extension Training (SET) Office and the Admissions Office are responsible for marketing distance education courses.
    -- Seminary

* A variety of people are responsible for marketing distance education courses -- each academic division, distance learning administrators, and college relations.
    -- Senior College with between 5,000 and 15,000 students

* The director of distance education working with the News and Information Services Coordinator on campus and is responsible for marketing distance education courses.
    -- University with fewer than 5,000 students

* The Director of Distance Education is responsible for marketing distance education courses.
    -- Senior College with fewer than 5,000 students

* Continuing Professional Education's Director of Marketing is responsible for marketing distance education courses.
    -- Junior College with between 5,000 and 15,000 students

* Extended Learning is responsible for marketing distance education courses.
    -- Senior College with between 5,000 and 15,000 students

* The Telecourse Coordinator and the PR Office are responsible for marketing distance education courses.
    -- Senior College with more than 15,000 students

* Programs and the college's marketing department are responsible for marketing distance education courses.

* The University has a contract for marketing with Canter Educational Productions in Santa Monica, CA.

* The individual programs and their departments are responsible for marketing distance education courses.
    -- University with more than 15,000 students

* Marketing and Media are responsible for marketing distance education courses.
    --Junior College

* The Division of Adult Learning is responsible for marketing distance education programs.
    -- Senior College

* Directors of telelearning, and distance learning are responsible for marketing distance education programs.

* All extended campuses are responsible for marketing distance education courses.

* The Director of Distance Education and the Public Relations Officer, are both responsible for marketing distance education courses.

CHAPTER SEVEN: PROFITABILITY AND REVENUES IN DISTANCE EDUCATION

40% of distance education programs operate at a loss. 25% of such programs operate with a profit margin of less than 10% above costs while another 25% operate with a profit margin between 11% and 30% above costs. 10% of distance education programs earn between 31% and 50% above costs. The data in this section must be considered a rough approximation of reality since the term "profitability" did not appear to be uniformly interpreted by all respondents. By profitability, we mean the extent to which all revenues exceed all costs, both marginal and fixed. However, public colleges did not always appear to fully consider the full impact of state subsidies, and overhead expenses were not uniformly accounted for by all parties. Since much of higher education is not "profitable" in the private sector sense, it is best to think of the following data in light of how this term is generally understood in an academic context. Our best estimate derived from follow up interviews is that profitability in the sense understood here is perhaps best approximated by the term "cash flow." However, some parties understood the term in its fullest sense, reflecting all attributed costs and subsidies.

Table #79: The Profit Margin--The Extent That Revenues Exceed Costs of Distance Education Programs

Status	Percentage of Colleges in the Sample
Less than 10%	25%
From 11% to 30%	25%
From 31% to 50%	10%
Greater Than 50%	0%
Loss	40%

Almost half of distance education programs with fewer than 250 or between 250 and 1,000 students enrolled operate at a loss. Distance education programs with more than 1,000 students enrolled, on the other hand, operate with a profit margin of 30% or less. The above data are shown in table #80 on the following page.

Primary Research Group, Inc.   P.O. Box 20853, New York, NY 10023   212/397-5055

Table #80: The Profit Margin--The Extent That Revenues Exceed Costs of Distance Education Programs, broken out by the number of students enrolled in the program.

Status	Less Than 250	Between 250 and 1,000	More Than 1,000
Less than 10%	22.2%	28.7%	50%
From 11% to 30%	33.3%	14.2%	50%
From 31% to 50%	0%	14.2%	0%
Greater Than 50%	0%	0%	0%
Loss	44.5%	42.9%	0%

Three quarters of distance education programs in the sample located in the South operate at a loss, while the remaining quarter operate with a profit margin of less than 10% above cost. One third of distance education programs in the Northeast operate at a loss, while one third operates with a profit margin of less than 10% above cost and the final third operates with a profit margin between 11% and 30% above costs. One fifth of the distance education programs in the Midwest operate at a loss, while two fifths operate with a profit margin between 11% and 30% above cost and the final two fifths operate with a profit margin between 31% and 50% above cost.One half of distance education programs in the West operate with a profit margin of less than 10% above cost while the other half operates with a profit margin between 11% and 30% above cost.

Table #81: The Profit Margin--The Extent That Revenues Exceed Costs of Distance Education Programs, broken out by the regional location of the college.

Status	West	South	Northeast	Midwest
Less than 10%	50%	25%	33.3%	0%
From 11% to 30%	50%	0%	33.3%	40%
From 31% to 50%	0%	0%	0%	40%
Greater Than 50%	0%	0%	0%	0%
Loss	0%	75%	33.3%	20%

Primary Research Group, Inc.   P.O. Box 20853, New York, NY 10023   212/397-5055

73

One third of junior colleges, and almost half of senior colleges, operate at a loss. One third of junior colleges in the sample operate with a profit margin of less than 10% above cost, while the remaining third operates with a margin between 11% and 50% above cost. Almost a fifth of other colleges operate with a profit margin of less than 10% above cost while less than two fifths operates with a margin between 11% and 30% above cost.

Table #82: The Profit Margin--The Extent That Revenues Exceed Costs of Distance Education Programs, broken out by the level of the college, junior or senior.

Status	Junior Colleges	Senior Colleges
Less than 10%	33.3%	18.1%
From 11% to 30%	11.1%	36.4%
From 31% to 50%	22.2%	0.0%
Greater Than 50%	0.0%	0.0%
Loss	33.3%	45.5%

CHAPTER EIGHT: TEACHERS AND STUDENTS IN DISTANCE EDUCATION

42.5% of colleges with established distance education programs compensate instructors for course development on a regular basis; 47.5% do not. 10% of colleges with established distance education programs sometimes compensate DE instructors for course development. Course development in this sense does not mean teaching; it means preparing the course so that it can be taught in a distance learning context. The concept as so employed includes the preparation of course materials, adjustments to lectures and other details of making sure that course materials can be effectively presented over the internet, through a videoconference, on cable television or through any of the other means often used to conduct distance education. The costs, both in time and money, is one of the major impediments to the rapid development of distance education, and DE instructors often complain (apparently with some justification) that they must shoulder too much of the burden of adjusting course materials to new mediums. Larger, and more established programs tend to provide more help to instructors in converting traditional course materials to new mediums and developing new materials most suitable to those mediums.

Table #83: Percentage of Colleges That Compensate Distance Education Instructors For Course Development.

Status	Compensated	Not Compensated	Sometimes Compensated
For the Development of Technology Based Lessons	42.5%	47.5%	10%
For the Conversion of Existing Course Materials	40.0%	52.5%	7.5%

As shown in table #84 on the following page, 37.5% of colleges with less than 250 students enrolled in distance education compensate instructors on a regular basis for the development of technology based lessons, as do 57.1% of colleges with between 250 and 1,000 students and 50% of colleges with more than 1,000 students.

Table #84: Percentage of Colleges That Compensate Distance Education Instructors for the Development of Technology Based Lessons, broken out by the number of students enrolled in the program.

Compensation Status	Less Than 250 Students	Between 250 and 1,000 Students	More Than 1,000 Students
Compensated	37.5%	57.1%	50%
Not Compensated	56.5%	42.9%	0%
Sometimes Compensated	6%	0%	50%

A higher percentage of colleges in the South (53.8%) and in the Northeast (50%) compensate instructors on a regular basis for the development of technology based lessons. 41.7% of those in the Midwest and only 22.2% of those in the West compensate instructors on a regular basis for the same efforts.

Table #85: The Percentage of Colleges That Compensate Distance Education Instructors for the Development of Technology Based Lessons, broken out by the regional location of The college.

Status	West	South	Northeast	Midwest
Compensated	22.2%	53.8%	50%	41.7%
Not Compensated	44.5%	46.2%	33.3%	58.3%
Sometimes Compensated	33.3%	0%	16.7%	0%

Primary Research Group, Inc.   P.O. Box 20853, New York, NY 10023   212/397-5055

36.8% of junior colleges with established distance education programs compensate instructors on a regular basis for the conversion of existing materials to DE materials, while 42.9% of senior colleges compensate instructors on a regular basis for the same efforts.

Table #86: Percentage of Colleges That Compensate Distance Learning Instructors For The Conversion of Existing Course Materials, broken out by the level of the college, junior or senior.

Status	Junior Colleges	Colleges
Compensated	36.8%	42.9%
Not Compensated	57.9%	47.6%
Sometimes Compensated	5.3%	9.5%

37.5% of colleges with less than 250 students enrolled in distance education compensate instructors on a regular basis for the conversion of existing course materials to DE course materials. 57.1% of those with between 250 and 1,000 students and 50% of those with more than 1,000 students compensate instructors on a regular basis for the same efforts.

Table #87: Percentage of Colleges That Compensate Distance Education Instructors for the Conversion of Existing Course Materials, broken out by the number of students enrolled in the program.

Status	Less Than 250	Between 250 and 1,000	More Than 1,000
Compensated	37.5%	57.1%	50%
Not Compensated	56.2%	42.9%	25%
Sometimes Compensated	6.3%	0%	25%

Primary Research Group, Inc.   P.O. Box 20853, New York, NY 10023   212/397-5055

Higher percentages of surveyed colleges in the South (53.8%) and in the Midwest (50%) compensate instructors on a regular basis for the conversion for existing course materials to DE course materials. 22.2% of those in the West and only 16.7% of those in the Northeast compensated instructors on a regular basis for the same efforts.

Table #88: The Percentage of Colleges That Compensate Distance Education Instructors for the Conversion of Existing Course Material, broken out by the regional location of the college.

Status	West	South	Northeast	Midwest
Compensated	22.2%	53.8%	16.7%	50%
Not Compensated	55.6%	46.2%	66.6%	50%
Sometimes Compensated	22.2%	0%	16.7%	0%

36.8% of junior colleges with established distance education programs compensate instructors on a regular basis for the conversion of existing course materials to DE course materials while Only a slightly higher percentage of senior colleges, 42.9%. compensate instructors on a regular basis for the same efforts.

Table #89: Percentage of Colleges That Compensate Distance Education Instructors For The Conversion of Existing Course Materials, broken out by the level of the college, junior or senior.

Status	Junior Colleges	Colleges
Compensated	36.8%	42.9%
Not Compensated	57.9%	47.6%
Sometimes Compensated	5.3%	9.5%

In 65.8% of colleges with an established distance education program, the teaching load of a DE instructor is the same as that of a traditional classroom instructor. It is higher than that of a traditional classroom instructor in 23.7% of colleges and lower in only 10.5% of colleges.

Table #90: Distance Education Instructor Teaching Loads Relative to Traditional Classroom Instructor Teaching Loads

Status	Colleges
Same As A Traditional Class	65.8%
Higher Than A Traditional Class	23.7%
Lower Than A Traditional Class	10.5%

Size of DE program and classroom teaching load for DE instructors appear largely unrelated, as shown in table #91 on the following page. The teaching load of a distance education instructor is the same as that of a traditional classroom instructor in 58.8% of colleges with fewer than 250 students enrolled in distance education, in 91.7% of colleges with between 250 and 1,000 students, and in 25% of those with more than 1,000 students.

It is higher than that of a traditional classroom instructor in 29.4% of colleges with fewer than 250 students, in 8.3% of colleges with between 250 and 1,000 students, and in 75% of those with more than 1,000 students.

It is lower than that of a traditional classroom instructor in 11.8% of colleges with fewer than 250 students, and in none of the colleges with between 250 and 1,000, or more than 1,000, students.

Table #91: Distance Education Instructor Teaching Loads, Relative to Traditional Classroom Instructor Teaching Loads, broken out by the number of students enrolled in the program.

Status	Less Than 250	Between 250 and 1,000	More Than 1,000
Same As A Traditional Class	58.8%	91.7%	25%
Higher Than A Traditional Class	29.4%	8.3%	75%
Lower Than A Traditional Class	11.8%	0%	0%

The teaching load of the distance education instructor is the same as that of a traditional classroom instructor in all of colleges located in the Northeast, in 66.7% of colleges located in the West, in 60% of those located in the Midwest, and in 53.8% of those located in the South.

It is higher than that of a traditional classroom instructor in none of the colleges located in the Northeast and with an established distance education program, in 22.2% of the colleges located in the West, in 20% of those located in the Midwest, and in 38.5% of those located in the South.

It is lower than that of a traditional classroom instructor in none of the colleges located in the Northeast and with an established distance education program, in 11.1% of the colleges located in the West, in 20% of those located in the Midwest, and in 7.7% of those located in the South.

Table #92: Distance Education Instructor Teaching Loads, Relative to Traditional Classroom Instructor Teaching Loads, broken out by the regional location of the college.

Status	West	South	Northeast	Midwest
Same As A Traditional Class	66.7%	53.8%	100%	60%
Higher Than A Traditional Class	22.2%	38.5%	0%	20%
Lower Than A Traditional Class	11.1%	7.7%	0%	20%

Primary Research Group, Inc.   P.O. Box 20853, New York, NY 10023   212/397-5055

The teaching load of a distance education instructor, relative to that of a traditional classroom instructor, appears to be unrelated to the level of the college as well. It is the same in 64.7% of junior colleges and in 66.7% senior colleges. It is higher in 23.5% of junior colleges and in 23.8% of senior colleges. And it is lower in 11.8% of junior colleges and 9.5% of senior colleges.

Table # 93: Distance Education Instructor Teaching Loads, Relative to Traditional Classroom Instructor Teaching Loads, broken out by the level of the college, junior or senior.

Status	Junior Colleges	Senior Year Colleges
Same As Traditional Class	64.7%	66.7%
Higher Than Traditional Class	23.5%	23.8%
Lower Than Traditional Class	11.8%	9.5%

Though the teaching load in distance education is often times the same as in the traditional classroom, DE instructors are required to undergo formal training in 54.8% of colleges with established distance education programs.

Table #94: Percentage of Colleges That Require Distance Education Instructors to Undergo Formal Training.

Status	Percentage of Colleges
Formal Training Required	54.8%
Formal Training Not Required	45.2%

81

Table 95: Percentage of Colleges That Require Distance Education Instructors to Undergo Formal Training, broken out by the number of students enrolled in the program.

Status	Less Than 250	Between 250 and 1,000	More Than 1,000
Formal Training Required	33.3%	85.7%	25%
Formal Training Not Required	66.7%	14.3%	75%

Table #96: The Percentage of Colleges That Require Distance Education Instructors to Undergo Formal Training, broken out by the regional location of the college.

Status	South	West	Northeast	Midwest
Formal Training Required	22.2%	57.1%	83.3%	61.5%
Formal Training Not Required	77.8%	42.9%	16.7%	38.5%

The level of the college does not seem to bear on whether or not formal training is required of the distance education instructor. It is required in 52.6% of junior colleges and in 56.5% of senior colleges.

Table #97: Percentage of Colleges That Require Distance Education Instructors to Undergo Formal Training, broken out by the level of the college, junior or senior.

Status	Junior College	College
Formal Training Required	52.6%	56.5%
Formal Training Not Required	47.4%	43.5%

Not too surprising, the percentage of students enrolled in distance education courses that receive training is somewhat smaller than that of instructors that receive training, 45.2% as opposed to 54.8%.

Table #98: The Percentage of Colleges in which Students Enrolled in Distance Education Courses Receive Training

Status	Percentage of Colleges
Receive Training	45.2%
Do Not Receive Training	54.8%

Students enrolled in distance education courses receive training in 38.9% of colleges with fewer than 250 students enrolled in such courses, in 64.3% of those with between 250 and 1,000 students, and in 25% of those with more than 1,000 students. For reasons not completely understood by us, it is teachers and students in the middle level programs that appear to receive the most training, more than those in the smaller and larger programs. Perhaps the larger programs already have a base of teachers and students sufficiently familiar with the technologies employed so that training is not necessary. Small programs may not have reached a suitable level of capitalization and institutional acceptance to command resources for training. It's a guess on our part. The above data are captured in table #99 on the following page.

Primary Research Group, Inc.   P.O. Box 20853, New York, NY 10023   212/397-5055

Table #99: The Percentage of Colleges in which Students Enrolled in Distance Education Courses Receive Training, broken out by the number of students enrolled in the program.

Status	Less Than 250	Between 250 and 1,000	More Than 1,000
Receive Training	38.9%	64.3%	25%
Do Not Receive Training	61.1%	35.7%	75%

The students receive training in 44.4% of colleges in the South, in 57.1% of colleges in the West, in 33.3% of those in the Northeast, and in 38.5% of those in the Midwest.

Table #100: The Percentage of Colleges in Which Students Enrolled in Distance Education Courses Receive Training, broken out by the regional location of the college.

Status	South	West	Northeast	Midwest
Receive Training	44.4%	57.1%	33.3%	38.5%
Do Not Receive Training	55.6%	42.9%	66.7%	61.5%

As indicated in table #101 on the following page, the percentage of students that receive training is much lower in junior colleges than in senior colleges, 26.3% in the former and 60.9% in the latter. This contrasts with the more even distribution of percentages in table #97, indicating the percentages of junior and senior colleges in which training is required of the instructor.

Table #101: The Percentage of Colleges in Which Students Enrolled in Distance Education courses Receive Training, broken out by the level of the college, junior or senior.

Status	Junior College	Senior College
Receive Training	26.3%	60.9%
Do Not Receive Training	73.7%	39.1%

67.5% of colleges with a distance education program have a formal evaluation program for distance education instructors.

Table #102: The Percentage of Colleges That Have a Formal Evaluation Program For Distance Education Instructors

Status	Percentage of Colleges
Formal Evaluation	67.5%
No Formal Evaluation	32.5%

50% of colleges with fewer than 250 students enrolled in a distance education program have a formal evaluation program for distance learning instructors, as do 92.3% of colleges with between 250 and 1,000 students enrolled in a distance education program and 50% of those with more than 1,000 students enrolled in such a program.

Table #103: The Percentage of Colleges That Have a Formal Evaluation Program For Distance Education Instructors, broken out by the number of students enrolled In the program.

Status	Less Than 250	Between 250 and 1,000	More Than 1,000
Formal Evaluation	50%	92.3%	50%
No Formal Evaluation	50%	7.7%	50%

50.0% of colleges located in the South have a formal evaluation program for distance education instructors, as do 78.6% of colleges located in the West, 60% of those located in the Northeast, and 50% of those located in the South.

Table #104: The Percentage of Colleges That Have a Formal Evaluation Program For Distance Education Instructors, broken out by the regional location of the college.

Status	South	West	Northeast	Midwest
Formal Evaluation	50%	78.6%	60%	69.2%
No Formal Evaluation	50%	21.4%	40%	30.8%

47.1% of junior colleges have a formal evaluation program for distance education instructors, while a full 82.6% of senior colleges have such an evaluation.

Table 105: The Percentage of Colleges That Have a Formal Evaluation Program For Distance Education Instructors, broken out by the level of the college, junior or senior.

Status	Junior College	College
Formal Evaluation	47.1%	82.6%
No Formal Evaluation	52.9%	17.4%

Interestingly, the percentage of Distance learning instructors that are adjuncts is lower than the percentage of adjuncts in the overall higher education teaching population. The mean percentage of distance education instructors that are adjunct faculty was 27.34%; the median 15%; the minimum 0%; the maximum 100%.

Table #106: The Percentage of Distance Education Instructors That Are Adjunct Faculty*.

Mean	Median
27.34%	15.00%

*In this case, adjunct means not a salaried teacher, a teacher employed on a course by course basis.

The mean percentage of distance education instructors that are adjunct faculty in schools with fewer than 250 students enrolled in distance education was 25.44%; the median 12.5%; the minimum 0%; the maximum 100%. For schools with between 250 and 1,000 students enrolled in distance education, the numbers are similar; the mean 22.77%; the median 10%; the minimum 0%; the maximum 85%. For schools with more than 1,000 students enrolled in distance education the mean was 21.2%; the median 11.5%; the minimum 2%; the maximum 60%.

Table #107: The Percentage of Distance Education Instructors That Are Adjunct Faculty, broken out by the number of students enrolled in the program.

Status	Mean	Median
Fewer Than 250	25.44%	12.5%
Between 250 and 1,000	22.77%	10.0%
More Than 1,000	21.20%	11.5%

Primary Research Group, Inc.   P.O. Box 20853, New York, NY 10023   212/397-5055

Table #108: The Percentage of Distance Education Instructors That Are Adjunct Faculty, broken out by the regional location of the college.

Status	Mean	Median
West	18.00%	20.0%
South	16.71%	7.5%
Northeast	53.30%	55.0%
Midwest	33.70%	25.0%

The percentage of distance education instructors at junior colleges that were adjunct faculty was not as high as one might expect. The mean percentage was 29.32%; the median 20.0%; the minimum 0.0%; and the maximum 100.0%. In contrast, the mean percentage at senior colleges was 25.64%; the median 12.5%; the minimum 0.0%; and the maximum 100.0%.

Table #109: The Percentage of Distance Education Instructors That Are Adjunct Faculty, broken out by the level of the college, junior or senior.

Status	Mean	Median	Minimum	Maximum
Junior Colleges	29.32%	20.0%	0.0%	100.0%
Senior Colleges	25.64%	12.5%	0.0%	100.0%

It was more common for colleges to draw on full-time staff to teach distance education courses. The mean percentage of DE instructors that were full-time staff was 65.05%; the median 80.00%.

Table #110: The Percentage of Distance Education Instructors That Are Full Time Staff

Mean	Median
65.05%	80.00%

Interestingly, the percentage of distance instructors that were full-time staff did not increase with the number of students enrolled in the program, as one might expect. The lowest percentage was in the programs with between 250 and 1,000 students, while those with fewer than 250 and more than 1,000 were about the same.

Table #111: The Percentage of Distance Education Instructors That Are Full Time Staff, broken out by the number of students enrolled in the distance education program.

Status	Mean	Median
Fewer Than 250	74.56%	87.50%
Between 250 and 1,000	60.00%	70.00%
More Than 1,000	78.7%	88.50%

The percentage of distance education instructors that were full-time faculty varied considerably from region to region. The mean percentage in the West was 82.0%; the median 80.0%; the minimum 50.0%; and the maximum 100.0%. The mean percentage in the South was 69.4%; the median 87.5%; the minimum 0.0%; and the maximum 100.0%. The mean percentage in the Northeast was 46.7%, the median 45.0%; the minimum 0.0%; and the maximum 100.0%. The mean percentage in the Midwest was 56.4%; the median 55.0%; the minimum 0.0%; and the maximum 100.0%. The above data are captured in table #112 on the following page.

Primary Research Group, Inc.   P.O. Box 20853, New York, NY 10023   212/397-5055

Table #112: The Percentage of Distance Education Instructors That Are Full Time Staff, broken out by the regional location of the college.

Status	Mean	Median	Minimum	Maximum
West	82.0%	80.0%	50.0%	100.0%
South	69.4%	87.5%	0.0%	100.0%
Northeast	46.7%	45.0%	0.0%	100.0%
Midwest	56.4%	55.0%	0.0%	100.0%

The mean percentage of distance education instructors at junior colleges that were full-time staff was 60.00%, and the median 70.0%. The mean percentage at senior colleges was 69.41%, and the median 82.5%. The minimum for both was 0.00%. The maximum for both was 100.0%.

Table #113: The Percentage of Distance Education Instructors That Are Full Time Staff, broken out by the level of the college, junior or senior.

Status	Mean	Median	Minimum	Maximum
Junior Colleges	60.00%	70.0%	0.00%	100.00%
Senior Colleges	69.41%	82.5%	0.00%	100.00%

The amount that distance education instructors are compensated for course development ranged from $0 to $5,000. The mean amount was $826, and the median $300.

Table #114: The Amount Distance Education Instructors Are Compensated For Course Development.

Mean	Median	Minimum	Maximum
$826.00	$300.00	$0.00	$5000.00

Primary Research Group, Inc.   P.O. Box 20853, New York, NY 10023   212/397-5055

The amount that DE instructors were compensated for course development differed with the number of students enrolled in the distance education program, but not as might be expected. The mean percentage for colleges with fewer than 250 students enrolled in the program was $770.00; the median; $0.00; the minimum $0.00; and the maximum $3,500. The mean percentage for colleges with between 250 and 1,000 students enrolled was $509; the median $300.00; the minimum $0.00; and the maximum $2,000. The mean percentage for colleges with more than 1,000 students enrolled was $3,750; the median $3,750; the minimum $2,500; and the maximum $5,000.

Table #115: The Amount Distance Education Instructors Are Compensated For Course Development, broken out by the number of students enrolled in the program.

Status	Mean	Median	Minimum	Maximum
Fewer Than 250	$770.00	$0.00	$0.00	$3500.00
Between 250 and 1,000	$509.00	$300.00	$0.00	$2000.00
More Than 1,000	$3750.00	$3,750.00	$2500.00	$5000.00

The amount that DE instructors are compensated for course development also varies, and sometimes considerably, from region to region. The mean amount for colleges in the sample located in the West was $790.00; the median $0.00; the minimum $0.00; and the maximum $2,500. The mean percentage for colleges located in the South was $1,277.00; the median $442.00; the minimum $0.00; and the maximum $5,000.00. The mean percentage for colleges located in the Northeast was $1,000.00; the median $250; the minimum $0.00; and the maximum $3,500; the mean percentage for colleges located in the Midwest was $300.00; the median $300; the minimum $0.00; and the maximum $900.00. The above data are shown in table #116 on the following page.

Table #116: The Amount Distance Education Instructors
Are Compensated For Course Development, broken out by the regional location of the college.

Status	Mean	Median	Minimum	Maximum
West	$790.00	$0.00	$0.00	$2,500.00
South	$1,277.00	$442.00	$0.00	$5,000.00
Northeast	$1,000.00	$250.00	$0.00	$3,500.00
Midwest	$300.00	$300.00	$0.00	$900.00

4-year colleges compensated instructors much more for course development than junior colleges. Mean compensation for course development at junior colleges was $526.00, and the median $0.00, the mean compensation at senior colleges was $1,100.00, and the median $500.00. The minimum and the maximum were the same, however. The former was $0.00 and the latter was $3,500.

Table #117: The Amount Distance Education Instructors Are Compensated For Course Development, broken out by the level of the college, junior or senior.

Status	Mean	Median	Minimum	Maximum
Junior Colleges	$526.00	$0.00	$0.00	$3,500.00
Senior Colleges	$1,100.00	$500.00	$0.00	$3,500.00

The amounts spent on training instructors for distance education are relatively modest. The mean percentage is $339.00; the median $75.00; the minimum $0.00; and the maximum $1,500.

Table #118: The Cost of Training Per Distance Education Instructor.

Mean	Median	Minimum	Maximum
$339.00	$75.00	$0.00	$1,500.00

Not surprisingly, the amount spent training each DE instructor increases with the number of students enrolled in the distance education program. The mean amount at colleges with fewer than 250 students enrolled in distance education was $185.00; the median $120.00; the minimum $0.00; and the maximum $500.00. The mean amount at colleges with between 250 and 1,000 students enrolled in DE courses was $550.00; the median $100.00; the minimum $50.00; and the maximum $1,500. The mean amount at colleges with more than 1,000 students was $1,000.00; the median $1,000.00; the minimum $1,000.00; and the maximum $1,000.00.

Table #119: The Cost of Training Per Distance Education Instructor, broken out by the number of students enrolled in the Program.

Number of Students Enrolled	Mean	Median	Minimum	Maximum
Fewer Than 250	$185.00	$120.00	$0.00	$500.00
Between 250 and 1,000	$550.00	$100.00	$50.00	$1,500.00
More Than 1,000	$1,000.00	$1,000.00	$1,000.00	$1,000.00

Also, the amount spent training each distance education instructor was considerably less at junior colleges than at senior colleges. Mean spending by junior colleges was $128.00; the median $40.00; the minimum $0.00; and the maximum $500.00. The mean amount at senior colleges was $551.00; the median $200.00; the minimum $3.00; and the maximum $1,500.

Table #120: The Cost of Training Per Distance Education Instructor, broken out by the level of the college, junior or senior.

Status	Mean	Median	Minimum	Maximum
Junior Colleges	$128.00	$40.00	$0.00	$500.00
Senior Colleges	$551.00	$200.00	$3.00	$1,500.00

Survey respondents were asked to briefly describe their training regimes for new distance education instructors. Their responses are listed below:

* Instructors using Interactive Classroom training in presentation, course adaptation and very general technical orientation to hardware are required to undergo formal training.
-- Junior College with more than 15,000 students

* Training for distance learning instructors consists of 6 hours of technical (hands-on) operation and teleteaching techniques.
-- Junior College

* Training for distance instructors consists of semi monthly meetings/workshops, summer workshop and an electronic chat room.
-- University with more than 15,000 students

* Training of distance educators consists of working with tech and academic support people.
-- Senior College

* Training of distance educators consists of a telephone conference call.
-- Graduate School

* Training for distance learning instructors consists of technical training in which they are taught to operating classroom equipment.
-- Junior College with fewer than 5,000 students

* Teacher training consists of asynchronous discussion, meetings, e-mail, and individual meetings.
-- Junior College with between 5,000 and 15,000 students

* Training for distance educators consists of TV use training, web use and web design training, and telecourse training, done in meetings.
-- University with between 5,000 and 15,000 students

* Training of distance educators is a 4 hour class session each semester offered by distance ed.
-- University with more than 15,000 students

* Distance learning instructor's training is 6-8 hours in distance learning classrooms.
-- Junior College with between 5,000 and 15,000 students

* Training for new distance learning instructors consists of a six hour block of theory and hands-on training.
-- Junior College with more than 15,000 students

* Training for new distance educators consists of a year long program administered by the Office of Distance Learning and supervised by the Vice President for Academic Affairs.
-- Senior College with fewer than 5,000 students

* Informal training for new distance education instructors consists of the use of tip sheets, visits to other distance ed. classes in progress, practice using the facility and software, consultations with others who have used the facility or software before, and consultations with the AV director and Director of Graduate Studies.
　　-- Senior College with fewer than 5,000 students

* Training for new distance educators consists of workshops for FrontPage. Faculty do their own web course design. There is a Learning Technologies Consultant to assist faculty in course design.
　　-- University with fewer than 5,000 students

* Training for new distance learning instructors consists of pedagogy, technology, and multi-media development.
　　-- University with fewer than 5,000 students

* Training for new distance learning instructors consists of production, performance, and evaluation techniques.
　　-- Junior College with between 5,000 and 15,000 students

* Training for new distance education instructors consists of a half day of training in pedagogy.
　　-- Junior College with between 5,000 and 15,000 students

* Training for new distance instructors consists of a 2 day workshop in which new instructors get hands on experience.

* Training for new distance learning instructors consists of an orientation to the program, in which students, the curriculum, the delivery system, and faculty roles and duties are discussed.

* Training for new distance learning instructors consists of an inhouse orientation.
　　-- University with more than 15,000 students

* Training for new distance learning instructors consists of 6 to 8 hours of instruction on pedagogy, technology, and copyright/fair use.

* Training for new distance learning instructors consists of 15 hours of training, including the development of one lesson and a presentation.

Almost nothing is spent on training students. As table #121 shows, no college spent more than $100.00 per student, most spent nothing and mean spending per student for DE training was $11.55.

Table #121: The Cost of Training Per Student in Distance Learning Programs.

Mean	Median	Minimum	Maximum
$11.55	$0.00	$0.00	$100.00

A few survey respondents described briefly described their training programs for students.

* Student training consists of an on-line tutorial for the web courses.
    -- University with between 5,000 and 15,000 students

* Student training consists of orientation during first class or during registration.
    -- University with more than 15,000 students

* Training for new distance education students consists of handouts and printed tips.
    -- Senior College with more than 15,000 students

Primary Research Group, Inc.   P.O. Box 20853, New York, NY 10023   212/397-5055

CHAPTER NINE: TECHNOLOGIES AND TECHNIQUES

Four general technological approaches predominate in the college distance learning market: 1) approaches that favor the internet, 2) those that favor live or tape broadcast/wire technologies (satellite, television, cable), 3) those that predominantly employ mail and phone correspondence often supplemented with audio and video tape, and 4) those that favor live videoconferencing. It appears that approaches that favor the internet, and those that favor live videoconferencing have the best prospects for the future.

Table #122: Summary of Program Technology Preferences.

TECHNOLOGY	Mean % of Sample that Employ as a Primary Vehicle
Mail Correspondence	19.95%
Fax	5.73%
Fax Broadcasting	2.78%
e-Mail Correspondence	17.61%
Internet	27.10%
Audio Cassette	3.90%
Live Audio	4.41%
Live Radio	0.0488%
Telephone	10.27%
Voice Mail	7.17%
Interactive Voice Response	5.00%
Videocassette	14.31%
Tape Video	17.80%
Tape Broadcast	9.07%
Tape Cablecast	9.76%
Tape Satellite	2.49%
Live Video	9.12%
Live Broadcast	2.93%

Live Cablecast	3.46%
Live Satellite	2.51%
Interactive Video	23.95%
Computer to Computer Videoconferencing	0.0488%
CD-ROM	0.61%

It appears that most classes relied upon one particular delivery system as their method of communication. Only one in five classes used a mix of two or more.

Table #123: Percentage of Distance Education Classes That Predominantly Employ a Mix of Two of More Delivery Systems as their Method of Communication

Mean	Median	Minimum	Maximum
20.33%	0%	0%	100%

Generally, respondents indicated that they intended to make greater use of the internet and e-mail, voice mail, telephone and fax technologies, as well as interactive and computer to computer videoconferencing technologies.

The percentage of colleges that plan to make greater use of mail correspondence as a method of communication in their distance education programs was 23%; lesser use 18%; no use 41%; and the same use 18%.

Table #124: Percentage of Colleges that Plan to Make Greater, Lesser, No, or the Same Use of Mail Correspondence As a Method of Communication in Their Distance Education Programs.

Greater Use	Lesser Use	No Use	Same Use
23%	18%	41%	18%

The percentage of colleges that plan to make greater use of fax as a method of communication in their distance education programs was 38.5%; lesser use 7.7%; no use 35.8%; and the same use 18%.

Table #125: Percentage of Colleges that Plan to Make Greater, Lesser, No, or the Same Use Fax As a Method of Communication in Their Distance Education Program.

Greater Use	Lesser Use	No Use	Same Use
38.5%	7.7%	35.8%	18%

The percentage of colleges that plan to make greater use of fax broadcasting as a method of communication in their distance education programs was 7.9%; lesser use 7.9%; no use 73.7%; and the same use 10.5%.

Table #126: Percentage of Colleges that Plan to Make Greater, Lesser, No, or the Same Use of Fax Broadcasting As a Method of Communication in Their Distance Education Program.

Greater Use	Lesser Use	No Use	Same Use
7.9%	7.9%	73.7%	10.5%

The percentage of colleges that plan to make greater use of e-mail as a method of communication in their distance education programs was 75%; lesser use 2.5%; no use 10%; and the same use 12.5%.

Table #127: Percentage of Colleges that Plan to Make Greater, Lesser, No, or the Same Use E-Mail As a Method of Communication in Their Distance Education Program.

Greater Use	Lesser Use	No Use	Same Use
75%	2.5%	10%	12.5%

The percentage of colleges that plan to make greater use of the Internet (WEB and e-mail) as a method of communication in their distance education programs was 92.5%; lesser use 0%; no use 2.5%; and the same use 0.5%.

Table #128 Percentage of Colleges that Plan to Make Greater, Lesser, No, or the Same Use of the Internet (WEB and E-Mail) As a Method of Communication in Their Distance Education Program.

Greater Use	Lesser Use	No Use	Same Use
92.5%	0%	2.5%	0.5%

The percentage of colleges that plan to make greater use of audio cassette as a method of communication in their distance education programs was 7.7%; lesser use 12.8%; no use 61.5%; and the same use 17.9%.

Table #129: Percentage of Colleges that Plan to Make Greater, Lesser, No, or the Same Use Of Audio Cassette As a Method of Communication in Their Distance Education Program.

Greater Use	Lesser Use	No Use	Same Use
7.7%	12.8%	61.5%	17.9%

The percentage of colleges that plan to make greater use of live audio as a method of communication in their distance education programs was 12.8%; lesser use 2.6%; no use 71.8%; and the same use 12.9%.

Table #130: Percentage of Colleges that Plan to Make Greater, Lesser, No, or the Same Use Of Live Audio As a Method of Communication in Their Distance Education Program.

Greater Use	Lesser Use	No Use	Same Use
12.8%	2.6%	71.8%	12.8%

The percentage of colleges that plan to make greater use of live radio as a method of communication in their distance education programs was 2.6%; lesser use 5.1%; no use 87.2%; and the same use 5.1%.

Table #131: Percentage of Colleges that Plan to Make Greater, Lesser, No, or the Same Use Of Live Radio As a Method of Communication in Their Distance Education Program.

Greater Use	Lesser Use	No Use	Same Use
2.6%	5.1%	87.2%	5.1%

The percentage of colleges that plan to make greater use of live telephone as a method of communication in their distance education programs was 20.5%; lesser use 7.7%; no use 61.5%; and the same use 10.3%.

Table #132: Percentage of Colleges that Plan to Make Greater, Lesser, No, or the Same Use Of Live Telephone As a Method of Communication in Their Distance Education Program.

Greater Use	Lesser Use	No Use	Same Use
20.5%	7.7%	61.5%	10.3%

The percentage of colleges that plan to make greater use of voice mail as a method of communication in their distance education programs was 43.6%; lesser use 2.5%; no use 38.5%; and the same use 15.4%.

Table #133: Percentage of Colleges that Plan to Make Greater, Lesser, No, or the Same Use Of Voice Mail As a Method of Communication in Their Distance Education Program.

Greater Use	Lesser Use	No Use	Same Use
43.6%	2.5%	38.5%	15.4%

The percentage of colleges that plan to make greater use of interactive voice response as a method of communication in their distance education programs was 22.5%; lesser use 2.5%; no use 70%; and the same use 0.5%.

Table #134: Percentage of Colleges that Plan to Make Greater, Lesser, No, or the Same Use Of Interactive Voice Response As a Method of Communication in Their Distance Education Program.

Greater Use	Lesser Use	No Use	Same Use
22.5%	2.5%	70%	0.5%

The percentage of colleges that plan to make greater use of video cassette as a method of communication in their distance education programs was 36.8%; lesser use 7.9%; no use 34.2%; and the same use 21.1%.

Table #135: Percentage of Colleges that Plan to Make Greater, Lesser, No, or the Same Use Of Video Cassette As a Method of Communication in Their Distance Education Program.

Greater Use	Lesser Use	No Use	Same Use
36.8%	7.9%	34.2%	21.1%

The percentage of colleges that plan to make greater use of tape video as a method of communication in their distance education programs was 36.8%; lesser use 7.9%; no use 34.2%; and the same use 21.1%.

Table #136: Percentage of Colleges that Plan to Make Greater, Lesser, No, or the Same Use Of Tape Video As a Method of Communication in Their Distance Education Program.

Greater Use	Lesser Use	No Use	Same Use
23%	7.7%	59%	10.3%

The percentage of colleges that plan to make greater use of tape tv broadcast as a method of communication in their distance education programs was 30.8%; lesser use 5.1%; no use 56.4%; and the same use 7.7%.

Table #137: Percentage of Colleges that Plan to Make Greater, Lesser, No, or the Same Use Of Tape TV Broadcast As a Method of Communication in Their Distance Education Program.

Greater Use	Lesser Use	No Use	Same Use
30.8%	5.1%	56.4%	7.7%

The percentage of colleges that plan to make greater use of tape cablecast as a method of communication in their distance education programs was 35.9%; lesser use 2.6%; no use 56.4%; and the same use 5.1%.

Table #138: Percentage of Colleges that Plan to Make Greater, Lesser, No, or the Same Use Of Tape Cablecast As a Method of Communication in Their Distance Education Program.

Greater Use	Lesser Use	No Use	Same Use
35.9%	2.6%	56.4%	5.1%

The percentage of colleges that plan to make greater use of tape satellite as a method of communication in their distance education programs was 23.1%; lesser use 2.5%; no use 64.1%; and the same use 10.3%.

Table #139: Percentage of Colleges that Plan to Make Greater, Lesser, No, or the Same Use Of Tape Satellite As a Method of Communication in Their Distance Education Program.

Greater Use	Lesser Use	No Use	Same Use
23.1%	2.5%	64.1%	10.3%

The percentage of colleges that plan to make greater use of live video as a method of communication in their distance education programs was 28.9%; lesser use 2.6%; no use 63.2%; and the same use 5.3%.

Table #140: Percentage of Colleges that Plan to Make Greater, Lesser, No, or the Same Use Of Live Video As a Method of Communication in Their Distance Education Program.

Greater Use	Lesser Use	No Use	Same Use
28.9%	2.6%	63.2%	5.3%

The percentage of colleges that plan to make greater use of live tv broadcast as a method of communication in their distance education programs was 20.5%; lesser use 5.1%; no use 66.7%; and the same use 7.7%.

Table #141: Percentage of Colleges that Plan to Make Greater, Lesser, No, or the Same Use Of Live TV Broadcast As a Method of Communication in Their Distance Education Program.

Greater Use	Lesser Use	No Use	Same Use
20.5%	5.1%	66.7%	7.7%

The percentage of colleges that plan to make greater use of live cablecast as a method of communication in their distance education programs was 20.5%; lesser use 2.5%; no use 71.8%; and the same use 5.2%.

Table #142: Percentage of Colleges that Plan to Make Greater, Lesser, No, or the Same Use Of Live Cablecast As a Method of Communication in Their Distance Education Program.

Greater Use	Lesser Use	No Use	Same Use
20.5%	2.5%	71.8%	5.2%

The percentage of colleges that plan to make greater use of live satellite as a method of communication in their distance education programs was 23.7%; lesser use 2.6%; no use 68.4%; and the same use 5.3%.

Table #143: Percentage of Colleges that Plan to Make Greater, Lesser, No, or the Same Use Of Live Satellite As a Method of Communication in Their Distance Education Program.

Greater Use	Lesser Use	No Use	Same Use
23.7%	2.6%	68.4%	5.3%

The percentage of colleges that plan to make greater use of interactive video/videoconferencing as a method of communication in their distance education programs was 64.1%; lesser use 5.1%; no use 28.2%; and the same use 2.6%.

Table #144: Percentage of Colleges that Plan to Make Greater, Lesser, No, or the Same Use Of Interactive Video/Videoconferencing As a Method of Communication in Their Distance Education Program.

Greater Use	Lesser Use	No Use	Same Use
64.1%	5.1%	28.2%	2.6%

The percentage of colleges that plan to make greater use of computer to computer videoconferencing as a method of communication in their distance education programs was 59%; lesser use 2.6%; no use 38.4%; and the same use 0%.

Table #145: Percentage of Colleges that Plan to Make Greater, Lesser, No, or the Same Use Of Computer to Computer Videoconferencing As a Method of Communication in Their Distance Education Program.

Greater Use	Lesser Use	No Use	Same Use
59%	2.6%	38.4%	0%

The percentage of colleges that plan to make greater use of CD-ROM as a method of communication in their distance education programs was 59%; lesser use 2.6%; no use 38.4%; and the same use 0%.

Table #146: Percentage of Colleges that Plan to Make Greater, Lesser, No, or the Same Use Of CD-ROM Videoconferencing As a Method of Communication in Their Distance Education Program.

Greater Use	Lesser Use	No Use	Same Use
56.4%	0%	41%	2.6%

As stated above, it appears that colleges intend to employ the internet and live videoconferencing in the future, much more than any other delivery system.

Table #147: Summary Table of College Future Distance Learning Technology Usage Intentions.

TECHNOLOGY	Intend Greater Use	Intend Lesser Use
Mail Correspondence	23%	18%
Fax	38.5%	7.7%
Fax Broadcasting	7.9%	7.9%
e-Mail Correspondence	75%	2.5%
Internet	92.5%	0.0%
Audio Cassette	7.7%	12.8%
Live Audio	12.8%	2.6%
Live Radio	2.6%	5.1%
Telephone	20.5%	7.7%
Voice Mail	43.6%	2.5%
Interactive Voice Response	22.5%	2.5%

Videocassette	36.8%	7.9%
Tape Video	23%	7.7%
Tape Broadcast	30.8%	5.1%
Tape Cablecast	35.9%	2.6%
Tape Satellite	23.1%	2.5%
Live Video	28.9%	2.6%
Live Broadcast	20.5%	5.1%
Live Cablecast	20.5%	2.5%
Live Satellite	23.7%	2.6%
Interactive Video	64.1%	5.1%
Computer to Computer Videoconferencing	59%	2.6%
CD-ROM	56.4%	0.0%

CHAPTER TEN: SERVICES OFFERED BY DISTANCE EDUCATION PROGRAMS

One of the developing practical management issues in distance education is: to what extent and how should distance education students enjoy access to the facilities and services of the college? The answer to this often depends on whether or not distance education students are paying full or partial tuition, and whether or not it is simply practical to offer them such services. The tables below relate the extent to which current distance education programs include access to other college facilities and services. The questions were posed to degree-granting and non-degree-granting programs.

A full 73% of the colleges surveyed offered a catalog at a distance.

Table #148: Percentage of Colleges With Distance Education Programs That Offer A (Course) Catalog At A Distance.

Status	Offer Catalog	Do Not Offer Catalog
Percentage	73%	27%

59.5% of the colleges surveyed offered a timetable at a distance.

Table #149: Percentage of Colleges With Distance Education Programs That Offer A Timetable At A Distance.

Status	Offer Timetable	Do Not Offer Timetable
Percentage	59.5%	40.5%

The same percentage, 59.5%, of the colleges offered advising at a distance.

Table #150: Percentage of Colleges With Distance Education Programs That Offer Advising At A Distance.

Status	Offer Advising	Do Not Offer Advising
Percentage	59.5%	40.5%

Only 45.9% offered career planning at a distance.

Table #151: Percentage of Colleges With Distance Education Programs That Offer Career Planning At A Distance.

Status	Offer Career Planning	Do Not Offer Career Planning
Percentage	45.9%	54.1%

51.4% of the colleges made financial aid available from a distance.

Table #152: Percentage of Colleges With Distance Education Programs That Offer Financial Aid At A Distance.

Status	Offer Financial Aid	Do Not Offer Financial Aid
Percentage	51.4%	48.6%

70.3% of the colleges enabled students to register from a distance.

Table #153: Percentage of Colleges With Distance Education Programs That Offer Registration At A Distance.

Status	Offer Registration	Do Not Offer Registration
Percentage	70.3%	29.7%

59.5% of the colleges enabled students to pay from a distance.

Table #154: Percentage of Colleges With Distance Education Programs That Offer Payment At A Distance.

Status	Offer Payment	Do Not Offer Payment
Percentage	59.5%	40.5%

51.4% of the colleges offered bookstore access at a distance.

Table #155: Percentage of Colleges With Distance Education Programs That Offer Bookstore Access At A Distance.

Status	Offer Bookstore Access	Do Not Offer Bookstore
Percentage	51.4%	48.6%

Primary Research Group, Inc.   P.O. Box 20853, New York, NY 10023   212/397-5055

67.6% offered library reference at a distance.

Table #156: Percentage of Colleges With Distance Education Programs That Offer Library Reference At A Distance.

Status	Offer Library Reference	Do Not Offer Library Reference
Percentage	67.6%	32.4%

59.5% offered a library catalog at a distance.

Table #157: Percentage of Colleges With Distance Education Programs That Offer Library Catalog At A Distance.

Status	Offer Library Catalog	Do Not Offer Library Catalog
Percentage	59.5%	40.5%

Only 16.2% offered library CD-ROMs at a distance.

Table #158: Percentage of Colleges With Distance Education Programs That Offer Library CD-ROMs At A Distance.

Status	Offer Library CD-ROMs	Do Not Offer Library CD-ROMs
Percentage	16.2%	83.3%

Primary Research Group, Inc.   P.O. Box 20853, New York, NY 10023   212/397-5055

43.2% offered access to library on-line databases at a distance.

Table #159: Percentage of Colleges With Distance Education Programs That Offer Access to Library On-line Databases At A Distance.

Status	Offer Library On-line Databases	Do Not Offer Library On-line Databases
Percentage	43.2%	56.8%

45.9% offered posted grades at a distance.

Table #160: Percentage of Colleges With Distance Education Programs That Offer Access to Posted Grades At A Distance.

Status	Offer Grades	Do Not Offer Grades
Percentage	45.9%	54.1%

The same percentage, 45.9%, offered access to grades at a distance.

Table #161: Percentage of Colleges With Distance Education Programs That Offer Transcripts At A Distance.

Status	Offer Transcripts	Do Not Offer Transcripts
Percentage	45.9%	54.1%

54.1% of colleges offered internet access at a distance.

Table #162: Percentage of Colleges With Distance Education Programs That Offer Internet Access At A Distance.

Status	Offer Internet Access	Do Not Offer Internet Access
Percentage	54.1%	45.9%

51.4% offered e-mail access at a distance.

Table #163: Percentage of Colleges With Distance Education Programs That Offer E-Mail Access At A Distance.

Status	Offer E-Mail Access	Do Not Offer E-Mail Access
Percentage	51.4%	48.6%

35.1% of colleges surveyed made tutoring available from a distance.

Table #164: Percentage of Colleges With Distance Education Programs That Offer Tutoring At A Distance.

Status	Offer Tutoring	Do Not Offer Tutoring
Percentage	35.1%	64.9%

32.4% made study groups available from a distance.

Table #165: Percentage of Colleges With Distance Education Programs That Offer Study
Groups At A Distance.

Status	Offer Study Groups	Do Not Offer Study Groups
Percentage	32.4%	67.6%

Primary Research Group, Inc.   P.O. Box 20853, New York, NY 10023   212/397-5055

CHAPTER ELEVEN: COST BREAKDOWN

Survey respondents were asked to break down their total DE program costs into different subject cost categories, plus an "other" category. The results are presented below.

Table #166: Percentage breakdown of total costs of distance education programs.

Expenditure Category	Mean Percentage of Total Costs	Median Percentage of Total Costs
Administration & Oversite	15.73%	15.00%
Instructor/Tutor Salaries	37.21%	38.00%
Advertising & Promotion	6.64%	5.00%
Course Development or Purchase	12.69%	8.00%
Equipment	11.08%	10.00%
Teacher Training & Recruitment	3.788%	5.000%
Telecommunications Costs	16.42%	10.00%
Facilities (Buildings/Classrooms)	8.25%	5.00%

Note that the data in the table above is an average of the data of the individual programs so that the average costs of the small programs carry as much weight in the total calculated mean as the larger programs. Data is broken out by size of program in the following tables.

The breakdown of the cost data by size of program (as defined by the number of students enrolled in DE courses) shows distinctly the gains from economies of scale as program size increases, at least for cost factors such as advertising and promotion, administration, and course development and purchase.

The percentage of total costs of distance education attributed to administration and oversite was highest for the colleges with between 250 and 1,000 students enrolled in distance education, though only slightly higher than it was for colleges with fewer than 250 students. The mean percentage for the latter was 15.86%; the median 15.00%. The mean percentage for the former was 17.50%; the median 17.50%. The mean percentage for colleges with more than 1,000 students was 10.00%; the median 10.00%. The above data are captured in table #167 on the following page.

Table #167: Percentage of total costs of distance education programs attributed to administration and oversite, broken out by the number of students enrolled in the program.

Number of Students	Mean Percentage of Total Costs	Median Percentage of Total Costs
Less than 250	15.86%	15.00%
Between 250 and 1,000	17.50%	17.50%
More than 1,000	10.00%	10.00%

In general, a higher percentage of total costs of distance education programs were attributed to instructor or tutor salaries at colleges with more than 1,000 students enrolled in the program. The mean and the median percentage were both 57.50%. The mean percentage for colleges with less than 250 students was 35.00%; the median 27.50%. The mean percentage for colleges with between 250 and 1,000 students was 32.67%; the median 38.00%.

Table #168: Percentage of total costs of distance education programs attributed to instructor or tutor salaries, broken out by the number of students enrolled in program.

Number of Students	Mean Percentage of Total Costs	Median Percentage of Total Costs
Less than 250	35.00%	27.50%
Between 250 and 1,000	32.67%	38.00%
More than 1,000	57.50%	57.50%

A very small percentage of total costs of distance education was attributed to advertising and promotion, across the board. The mean percentage for colleges with less than 250 students enrolled in distance education was 9.71%; the median 10.00%. The mean percentage for colleges with between 250 and 1,000 students was 3.000%; the median 2.000%. The mean percentage for colleges with more than 1,000 students was 5.00%; the median 5.00%.

Table #169: Percentage of total costs of distance education programs attributed to advertising and promotion, broken out by the number of students enrolled in the program.

Number of Students	Mean Percentage of Total Costs	Median Percentage of Total Costs
Less than 250	9.71%	10.00%
Between 250 and 1,000	3.000%	2.000%
More than 1,000	5.00%	5.00%

Not surprisingly, the percentage of total costs of distance education attributed to course development or purchase generally decreased as the size of the program increased. The mean percentage for colleges with fewer than 250 students enrolled in distance education was 17.00%; the median 15.00%. The mean percentage for colleges with between 250 and 1,000 students was 10.40%; the median 4.00%; the mean percentage for colleges with more than 1,000 students was 5.00%; the median 5.00%.

Table #170: Percentage of total costs of distance education programs attributed to course development or purchase, broken out by the number of students enrolled in the program.

Number of Students	Mean Percentage of Total Costs	Median Percentage of Total Costs
Less than 250	17.00%	15.00%
Between 250 and 1,000	10.40%	4.00%
More than 1,000	5.00%	5.00%

The percentage of total costs of distance education did not vary considerably with the size of the program. The mean percentage for colleges with fewer than 250 students enrolled in distance education was 8.60%; the median 10.00%; the mean percentage for colleges with between 250 and 1,000 students was 14.00%; the median 10.00%. The mean percentage for colleges with more than 1,000 students was 10.00%; the median 10.00%.

Table #171: Percentage of total costs of distance education programs attributed to equipment, broken out by the number of students enrolled in the program.

Number of Students	Mean Percentage of Total Costs	Median Percentage of Total Costs
Less than 250	8.60%	10.00%
Between 250 and 1,000	14.00%	10.00%
More than 1,000	10.00%	10.00%

The percentage of total costs of distance education attributed to teacher training and recruitment remained in the lower regions for all colleges in the sample. The mean percentage for colleges with fewer than 250 students enrolled in distance education was 3.25%; the median 3.50%. The mean percentage for colleges with between 250 and 1,000 students was 4.75%; the median 5.00%. The mean percentage for colleges with more than 1,000 students was 2.0000%; the median 2.0000%.

Table #172: Percentage of total costs of distance education programs attributed to teacher training and recruitment, broken out by the number of students enrolled in the program.

Number of Students	Mean Percentage of Total Costs	Median Percentage of Total Costs
Less than 250	3.25%	3.50%
Between 250 and 1,000	4.75%	5.00%
More than 1,000	2.0000%	2.0000%

The percentage of total costs of distance education attributed to telecommunications was somewhat higher. The mean percentage for colleges with fewer than 250 students was 16.40%; the median 10.00%. The mean percentage for colleges with between 250 and 1,000 students was 20.00%; the median 20.00%. The mean percentage for colleges with more than 1,000 students was 7.50%; the median 7.50%.

Table #173: Percentage of total costs of distance education programs attributed to telecommunications, broken out by the number of students enrolled in the program.

Number of Students	Mean Percentage of Total Costs	Median Percentage of Total Costs
Less than 250	16.40%	10.00%
Between 250 and 1,000	20.00%	20.00%
More than 1,000	7.50%	7.50%

Interestingly, the total costs of distance education programs attributed to facilities was highest for colleges with between 250 and 1,000 students enrolled in distance education. The mean percentage for colleges with fewer than 250 students was 6.50%; the median 3.00%. The mean percentage for colleges with between 250 and 1,000 students was 11.67%; the median 10.00%. The mean percentage for colleges with more than 1,000 students was 5.0000%; the median 5.000%.

Table #174: Percentage of total costs of distance education programs attributed to facilities, that is, buildings and classrooms, broken out by the number of students enrolled in the program.

Number of Students	Mean Percentage of Total Costs	Median Percentage of Total Costs
Less than 250	6.50%	3.00%
Between 250 and 1,000	11.67%	10.00%
More than 250	5.0000%	5.0000%

In general, the percentage of total costs of distance education attributed to administration and oversite, for junior colleges, is more than half of that for senior colleges. The mean percentage for junior colleges is 10.38%; the median 7.50%. The mean percentage for senior colleges is 21.86%; the median 20.00%.

Table #175: Percentage of total costs of distance education programs attributed to administration and oversite, broken out by the level of the college, junior or senior.

Type	Mean Percentage of Total Costs	Median Percentage of Total Costs
Junior Colleges	10.38%	7.50%
Senior Colleges	21.86%	20.00%

The percentage of total costs of distance education attributed to instructor or tutor salaries is high for both junior and senior colleges, though it is somewhat higher for the former. The mean percentage or junior colleges is 40.86%; the median 50.00%. The mean percentage for senior colleges is 33.57%; the median 30.00%.

Table #176: Percentage of total costs of distance education programs attributed to instructor or tutor salaries, broken out by the level of the college, junior or senior.

Type	Mean Percentage of Total Costs	Median Percentage of Total Costs
Junior Colleges	40.86%	50.00%
Senior Colleges	33.57%	30.00%

In contrast, as indicated in table #177 on the following page, the percentage of total costs of distance education attributed to advertising is low for both junior and senior colleges. The mean percentage for junior colleges is 5.50%; the median 5.00%. The mean percentage for senior colleges is 8.17%; the median 7.50%.

Table #177: Percentage of total costs of distance education programs attributed to advertising and promotion, broken out by the level of the college, junior or senior.

Type	Mean Percentage of Total Costs	Median Percentage of Total Costs
Junior Colleges	5.50%	5.00%
Senior Colleges	8.17%	7.50%

The mean percentage of total costs of distance education attributed to course development or purchase, for junior colleges, was 14.63%; the median 11.50%. For senior colleges, the mean percentage was 9.60%; the median 3.00%.

Table #178: Percentage of total costs of distance education programs attributed to course development or purchase, broken out by the level of the college, junior or senior.

Type	Mean Percentage of Total Costs	Median Percentage of Total Costs
Junior Colleges	14.63%	11.50%
Senior Colleges	9.60%	3.00%

The percentage of total costs of distance education attributed to equipment was similar for junior and senior colleges. The mean percentage for the former was 11.67%; the median 12.50%. The mean percentage for the latter was 10.50%; the latter 7.50%.

Table #179: Percentage of total costs of distance education programs attributed to equipment, broken out by the level of the college, junior or senior.

Type	Mean Percentage of Total Costs	Median Percentage of Total Costs
Junior Colleges	11.67%	12.50%
Senior Colleges	10.50%	7.50%

The percentage of total costs of distance education attributed to teacher training and recruitment hovered in the lowest five percent for both junior and senior colleges, though for the latter in was almost nothing. The mean percentage for junior colleges was 4.500%; the median 5.000%. The mean percentage for senior colleges was 2.33%; the median 1.00%.

Table #180: Percentage of total costs of distance education programs attributed to teacher training and recruitment, broken out by the level of the college, junior or senior.

Type	Mean Percentage of Total Costs	Median Percentage of Total Costs
Junior Colleges	4.500%	5.000%
Senior Colleges	2.33%	1.00%

The percentage of total costs of distance education attributed to telecommunications was somewhat higher for junior colleges than it was for senior colleges. The mean percentage for the former was 18.33%; the median 17.50%. The mean percentage for the latter was 14.50%; the median 10.00%.

Table #181: Percentage of total costs of distance education programs attributed to telecommunications, broken out by the level of the college, junior or senior.

Type	Mean Percentage of Total Costs	Median Percentage of Total Costs
Junior Colleges	18.33%	17.50%
Senior Colleges	14.50%	10.00%

The percentage of total costs of distance education attributed to facilities was relatively low, for both junior and senior colleges. The mean percentage for junior colleges was 6.25%; the median 5.00%. The mean percentage for senior colleges was 10.25%; the median 10.50%.

Table #182: Percentage of total costs of distance education programs attributed to facilities, that is, buildings and classrooms, broken out by the level of the college, junior or senior.

Type	Mean Percentage of Total Costs	Median Percentage of Total Costs
Junior Colleges	6.25%	5.00%
Senior Colleges	10.25%	10.50%

APPENDIX I: THE DISTANCE EDUCATION QUESTIONNAIRE

The full questionnaire is reproduced below.

DISTANCE EDUCATION QUESTIONNAIRE AND SURVEY INVITATION REQUEST

Primary Research Group, Inc., a publisher of surveys, monographs and research reports, is planning to publish a survey of administrators of distance education programs. We invite you to participate in our survey by filling out the survey form in exchange for a free copy of the report when it is published. The information that you provide is absolutely confidential; all data is amalgamated in a statistical package; no data is presented for individual institutions.

Primary Research is listed in Literary Market Place, the Findex Directory, Gale's Directory of Telecommunications Consultants and other standard directories. It is the publisher of "The Academic Library Budget & Expenditure Report", "Forecasting College & University Revenues" and other studies.

E-MAIL: Primarydat@AOL.COM

FAX: 212-397-5056

PHONE: 212-397-5055

MAILING ADDRESS: PO Box 20853/Columbus Circle Station/New York, New York 10023-1489

PHYSICAL ADDRESS: 30 west 63'rd street/New York, New York 10023

RETURN THE QUESTIONNAIRE BY JULY 10, 1997 to qualify for your free copy.

Send the questionnaire by fax, E-Mail or by mail.

What is the NAME and ADDRESS of your college:
CONTACT NAME:
PHONE NUMBER:
ADMINISTRATIVE/ORGANIZATIONAL PLANNING

1) At what level are distance education administrators in the hierarchy of the institution or organization (check one or more)

executive administration_____
traditional departmental administration____
faculty_____
Other (specify)_____

2) Who do distance education administrators report to in your organization?

academic department chairmen____
university administration_____
special distance learning department____
Other_____

3) Does your organization expect to expand its distance education offerings within the next year?

yes____no_____unsure_____

4) If your organization does plan to expand its distance education offerings, on a scale of 1-10 (with one rank as very important and 10 as unimportant), which reasons of those listed below are most important

To meet greater demand
stay competitive
serve new markets
provide alternatives to traditional student
reduce impact on college facilities
enhance the learning experience
help students become technology literate

5) How many distance education courses does your institution offer?_____

6) How many students are enrolled in distance education courses at or through your institution?_____

7) Does your organization offer a full degree program through distance education?

7b) If so, what degree(s)?

Primary Research Group, Inc.   P.O. Box 20853, New York, NY 10023   212/397-5055

8) Does your organization collect demographic information on students? (i.e. age, sex, income level of student, field of study?)
8b) If possible, briefly describe the demographic differences, if any, between distance learning students and students enrolled in more traditional courses of study?

9) Who is responsible for marketing distance education courses?

10) Are the courses marketed only to students of your organization?

11) Is distance education predominantly viewed by your organization as:

a) a profit-making function_____   b) an integral part of your traditional degree programs_____   c) a way to serve special populations_____e)other_____

MARKETING/BUSINESS

12) Does your organization's distance learning program or services serve a: local market_____ statewide market _____ national market _____ international market _____

13) Does your organization try to sell or license distance learning services to other organizations_____ or restrict the service to your own institution _____?

14) Has your organization ever sold a distance learning course to an organization in a developing country? _____

15) Has your organization ever sold a distance learning course to an organization in any foreign country_____?

16) Does your organization make any efforts (such as conducting market research) to assess market demand for distance learning courses? _____

17) Is the DE effort self supporting?_____

18) Does revenue from the DE courses under your administration go to: a) a traditional academic department____   b) an adult or continuing education program_____   c) A separate unit devoted to distance learning_____   d) the university administration_____   e) other (please specify)

19) About how much did your organization spend to market and advertise its distance education courses within the past year?

HARDWARE AND SOFTWARE

20 Does your organization offer any of the following services at a distance (check the appropriate delivery modes for each service): internet/web, phone/voice processing, e-mail and postal mail.

	Internet/Web	Phone/Voice Processing	E-Mail	Mail	Fax
Catalog					
Timetable					
Advising					
Career Planning					
Financial Aid					
Registration					
Payment					
Bookstore					
Library					
Reference					
Library Catalog					
Library CD-ROM's					
Library On-Line Databases					
Grades					
Transcripts					
Internet Access					
E-Mail Access					
Tutoring					
Study Groups					

21) How many students took a distance learning class at or through your institution in the last semester?

22) What percentage of distance learning classes are predominately: (check the percentage of your distance learning classes that employ the technique or technology listed)

     mail correspondence_____
     fax_____
     fax broadcasting_____
     e-mail correspondence_____
     Internet correspondence (WEB and e-mail)_____
     audio cassette_____
     live audio_____
         radio_____
         telephone_____
     voice mail_____
     interactive voice response_____
     video cassette_____

tape video_____
      broadcast_____
      cablecast_____
      satellite_____
live video _____
      broadcast_____
      cablecast_____
      satellite_____
interactive video_____
computer to computer videoconferencing_____
CD-ROM_____
mix of two or more delivery systems (CD-ROM, e-mail)_____

FACULTY

23) What percentage of distance education instructors are adjunct faculty?

24) What percentage of distance education instructors are full time staff?

25) Do instructors get paid (check all that apply)

    part of load
    overload
    per student
    as adjunct

26) Are instructors compensated for

    development of technology based lessons _____
    conversion of existing course materials_____

27) If so, how much are instructors compensated for course development?

28) Are distance instructors's teaching load:
    same as traditional class
    higher than traditional class
    lower than traditional class

29) Are new distance learning instructors required to undergo formal training in distance leaning?

30) If so, what does this training consist of?

31) Approximately how much does training cost per instructor?

32) Do students enrolled in distance learning courses receive any training?

33) If so, how much does the training cost, per student?

34) Does your organization have a formal evaluation program for distance educators?

35) What support services are offered to faculty designing courses for distance ed? ie. instructional designers, graphic artists, html programmers, etc.

36) Are courses designed in a) some kind of centralized facility. b) through grants to faculty, c) purchased from outside source, or 4) some other way (please define).

RACE, GENDER, CLASS, AND OTHER DEMOGRAPHIC INFORMATION

37) Please compare the student body demographics of your distance learning classes to those of similar classes taught in more traditional classroom settings, and answer the following questions. Some of the questions you may not be able to answer, but make reasonable estimates whenever possible:

Demographic Category	Percentage in DE Classes	Percentage in Comparable Traditional Classes
Hispanic American		
African American		
Female		
Disabled		
Over Age 35		
Over Age 50		

FINANCES

38) If your distance learning program is designed to enhance college revenues, what would you say is the profit margin (the extent in percentage terms that revenues exceed costs)

a) less than 10%   b) from 11% to 30%   c) 31% to 50%   d) greater than 50%   e) loss

39) If possible, please provide an exact figure for the profit margin percentage.

40) Please specify in percentage terms how much of total distance education program costs the following expenditure categories account for:

Expenditure Category	Percentage of Total Costs
Administration & Oversight	
Instructor/Tutor Salaries	
Advertising & Promotion	
Course Development/Purchase	
Equipment	
Teacher Training & Recruitment	

Telecommunications Costs
Facilities (buildings/classrooms)
Other

41) Please indicate whether in your distance education program that you intend to make greater, lesser, or no use of the practices and technologies listed below

        mail correspondence_____
        fax_____
        fax broadcasting_____
        e-mail correspondence_____
        Internet correspondence (WEB and e-mail)_____
        audio cassette_____
        live audio_____
                radio_____
                telephone_____
        voice Mail_____
        interactive voice response_____
        video cassette_____
        tape video_____
                tv broadcast_____
                cablecast_____
                satellite_____
        live video _____
                tv broadcast_____
                cablecast_____
                satellite_____
        interactive video/videoconferencing_____
        computer to computer videoconferencing_____
        CD-ROM_____

APPENDIX II: REPORTS OF INTEREST FROM PRIMARY RESEARCH GROUP, INC.

The Adult and Continuing Education Business Report(isbn #: 1-57440-007-X)
(Price: $295.00/$95.00 for accredited academic institutions) Published in September 1997

This special report looks closely at trends in adult and continuing education in the United States, imparting essential planning information for strategic development. The report helps administrators to forecast the best areas for future growth, and forecast general trends in adult education spending. Profiles college and private sector adult education programs. Gives market demographic data on who takes what kind of adult education classes.

Restructuring Higher Education: Cost Containment and Productivity Enhancement Efforts of North American Colleges and Universities (isbn# 1-57440-006-1)
(Price: $59.50) Published in June 1997

This monograph looks closely at the cost containment and restructuring efforts of North American colleges and universities. Among the many issues discussed: trends in the employment of adjuncts, departmental reorganizations, use of new technologies such as advanced database software and the internet, the politics of administrative downsizing, cooperation among colleges to enhance bargaining power with suppliers in purchasing, "performance contracting", electric power procurement, telecommunications services procurement, 'speeded up" three year degrees, outsourcing of student services such as food service and residence halls, and many other issues of interest to college administrators.

Forecasting College and University Revenues (isbn#1-57440-003-7)
(Price: $130.00/$65.00 for accredited educational institutions) Published in April 1997

This special report examines the income outlook for American colleges and universities, exploring trends in overall enrollment, tuition, licensing, and endowment income, for profit college services, foreign student enrollment, state local and federal government support, and research income. Includes time series data on US consumer spending for higher education over the past 15 years.

The Academic Library Budget & Expenditure Report (isbn#1-57440-027-4)
(Price: $125.00/$70.00 for accredited educational institutions) Published October 1996

This special report is designed to give academic librarians insight into the materials and technology purchasing plans of America's two-year, four year and university academic libraries. The data in the report is based on 100 randomly chosen academic libraries in North America; data is presented on a per student basis, as well as in the aggregate, and broken out by size and type of library to allow for easy benchmarking and comparisons. Among the data categories: spending for journals, cataloging systems, CD-ROM, computer hardware, online services, books, salaries, etc. Also explores issues such as personnel benefits, internet usage patterns, seminar attendance and other issues of interest to academic librarians.

ORDER FORM

HOW TO ORDER: FAX THIS PAGE TO: 212-397-5056
E-MAIL US AT: Primarydat@AOL.COM
CALL US AT: 212-397-5055
Mail your order to: Primary Research Group, Inc.
PO Box 20853
New York, New York 10023

PUBLICATION	Unit Price	Quantity	Total Price

Name:

Institution:

Address:

| City | State/Province | Zip |

Phone Number:

Please Charge my credit card#_____ Expiration date_____

Bill me_____ Bill with the following PO#:_____

Shipping Charges

ADD $5.00 for the first volume and $2.00 for each subsequent volume for shipping in the continental USA. $10.00 for shipping first volume to Canada, Alaska and Hawaii ($3.00 per additional volume); $20.00 to all other destinations for first volume ($4.00 for each additional volume).